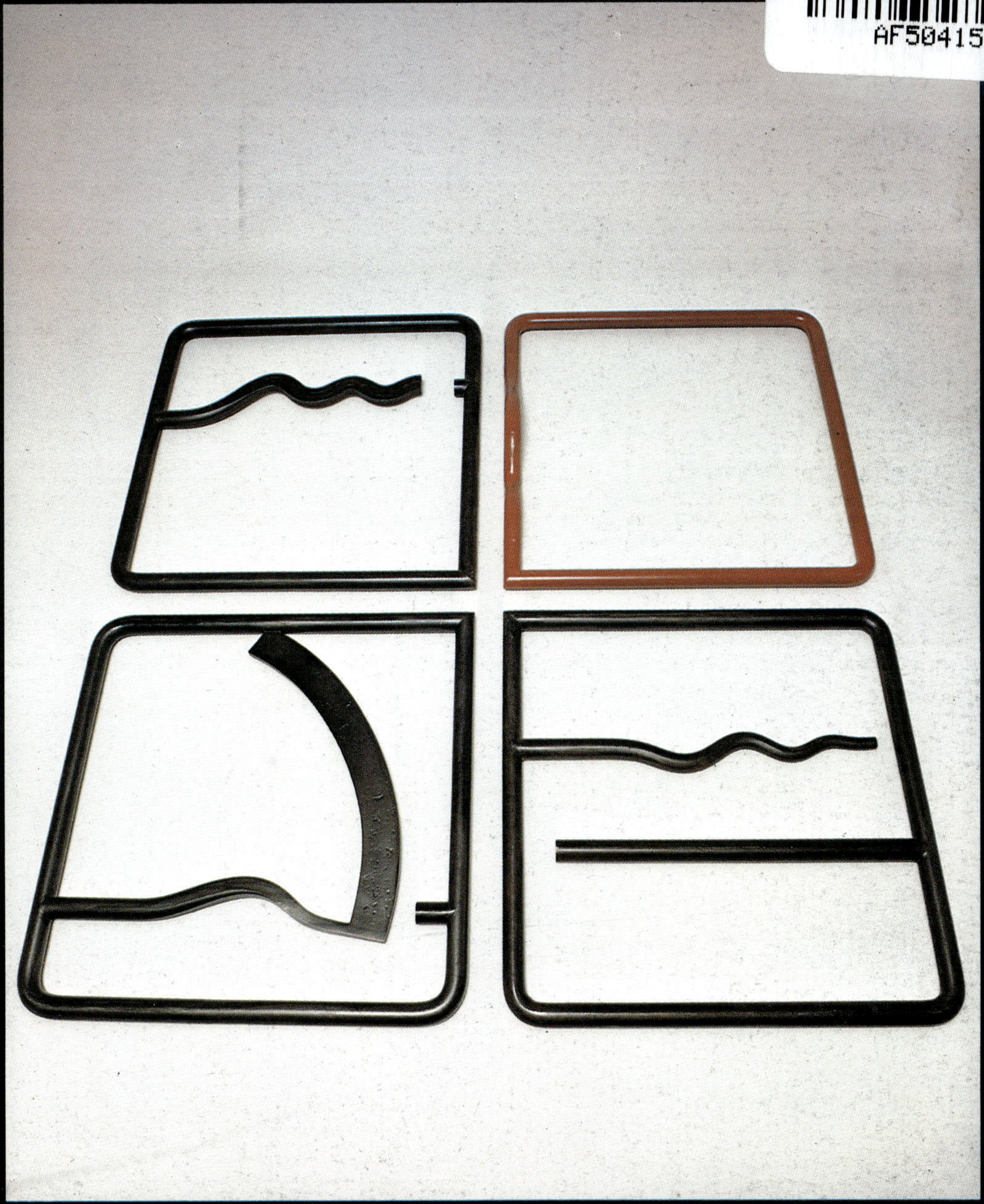

TOWARDS A NEW IRON AGE

MAY 12th–JULY 10th 1982

VICTORIA
& ALBERT
MUSEUM

Acknowledgements

The Museum would like to thank the following for their help with the exhibition: the many craftsmen who contributed pieces to it, and all those who have generously allowed us to borrow items from their collections.

The Selection Committee, for their initial choice of the exhibits, which has had to be emended owing to shortage of space and funds: James Horrobin, Giuseppe Lund, Anthony Robinson, Richard Quinnell; from the Crafts Council, Victor Margrie and Caroline Pearce-Higgins; and from the V & A., Claude Blair and Marian Campbell.

Paul Williams and Hamish Muir for designing the exhibition display and graphics; Antonio Bennetton, Dorothy Bosomworth, Caroline Pearce-Higgins and Richard Quinnell for contributing essays to the catalogue; Mike Kitcatt, Stanley Eost and Peter Macdonald for undertaking much of the photography, often under trying conditions; Michael Darby, Garth Hall, Eric Turner and the department of Metalwork for their stalwart help in putting up the exhibition; Shirley Bury and Barbara Cartlidge for their advice on jewellery; Griselda Gilroy and Susan Wilkin of the Crafts Council, the staff of the libraries of the Goldsmiths Hall, the R.I.B.A., Julie Laird and Sally Ready of the V & A Friends, and Alan Dingle and Hanspeter Lanz for much help and advice; Jim Wallace, without whose organising energy no North American Tour could have been attempted; and the Press Office at the V & A.

We should also like to acknowledge with gratitude the financial assistance received from the First National Bank of Memphis, Tennessee, USA (grant made under the First Bravo Program to enable the exhibition to tour the USA), the Worshipful Company of Armourers and Brasiers, the Worshipful Company of Blacksmiths, the Worshipful Company of Cutlers, the Worshipful Company of Ironmongers, the Artist-Blacksmiths' Association of North America and the Friends of the V & A.

© *Crown copyright 1982*
first published 1982

ISBN 0 905209 23 0
Dd. 8219681

Typeset by Hugh Wilson Typesetting, Norwich
Printed in England for Her Majesty's Stationery
Office by Commercial Colour Press Ltd, London.

The exhibition will travel to the following
places in the United States
between the autumns of 1982 and 1983:
Metal Museum, Memphis, Tennessee.
Flint Institute, Flint, Michigan.
Southern Illinois University, Carbondale, Ill.
Mint Museum, Charlotte, North Carolina.
American Craft Museum, New York.

Contents

Colour Plates

Frontispiece   David Watkins "Four Structures" 1981. Mild steel, partly coloured. Approximately 76cm square.

Reverse of frontispiece   Alfred Habermann "Gates from Trest", Czechoslovakia. Approximately 260 x 250cm.

Page 15   Stuart Hill "Blue Fence" 1980. Mild steel tube, painted. 4 metres long.

Page 16 (left to right).

Ruth Stourton, Pins, 1980. Steel, blued and inlaid with gold and silver. Each approximately 13cm long.

Robert Legg, Hand mirror, 1978. Mild steel, blued and inlaid with gold. 7.4cm diameter.

Malcolm Appleby, "Hawk ring" 1967-68. Mild steel, inlaid with gold and silver. 3.8cm maximum diameter.

Front Cover

Achim Kühn "Schwinginder Stahl". Steel and hardened high grade steel. 2.3m x 5m.

Back Cover

Alfred Habermann using a power hammer.

Preface

This is the first international display of wrought ironwork ever to be seen in this country. That it is staged in the V & A is appropriate not only because the museum houses what must be one of the most important collections of wrought iron in the world, but because of its commitment to contemporary exponents of the craft. The visitor will, for the first time, be able to see what has been achieved in the last few years and, hopefully, will be moved to think of the future potential of the art. Recently commissions have come not only from private individuals but also from public institutions, among them the Dean and Chapter of St. Paul's, Hampshire County Council and the V & A itself. These have all commissioned fine gates by British blacksmiths over the last two years. But these are only beginnings of what we hope will be an imaginative re-thinking of the use and potential of wrought iron as an art form.

Once again it is my pleasure to record a happy collaboration with the Crafts Council, whose encouragement of the craft of blacksmithing in recent years has nurtured this incipient renaissance. Particular thanks are also due to Giuseppe Lund, one of the exhibiting blacksmiths whose enthusiasm inspired the staging of the exhibition. My gratitude to my colleagues in the Department of Metalwork, in the case of this exhibition especially to Claude Blair, the Keeper, and Marian Campbell, is as always unstinted.

Sir Roy Strong,
Director

Foreword

Working iron and steel at red to near-white heat is a seductive experience; the metal becomes responsive in a manner totally inconceivable when it is cold. It seems impossible that this intractable material should yield such plasticity. The fire weld, executed with split second timing, is workmanship of risk at its most daring: balance, poise, physical energy and mental agility perfectly co-ordinated. Yet, forged iron has for much of the twentieth-century remained in the grip of historical pastiche or worse, ill digested modernism of the most banal kind. Certainly, there have been isolated examples of sensitive and generous work, mostly springing from the influence of the Arts and Crafts Movement, including that of Charles Rennie Mackintosh, but however glorious these individual creative statements there is no evidence of sustained aesthetic development. The past, while providing inspiration, has contributed to the craft's decline.

During the summer of 1979 and 1980 the Crafts Council organised two international workshops which brought together smiths with a broad range of experience and expertise. In their wake came a new confidence and a reaffirmation of forged iron as an expressive medium. Major commissions were undertaken for St. Paul's Cathedral, The Great Hall, Winchester, and the Victoria and Albert Museum itself. Two colleges of art are now offering degree courses with ironwork options. However, this ferment of activity has created a new set of problems. It has demanded a period of difficult, and often painful, reassessment with the artist blacksmiths struggling to establish a new identity. Almost inevitably the emerging confidence has on occasions been devalued by conceit, but it would be strange if it were to be otherwise during a time of rapid change. Such questioning is necessary to provide a sounder base for development.

If this development is to come about the impetus must be maintained, but it will need vigilance on the part of the blacksmiths themselves to see that innovation does not lightly dismiss good practice, both in design and making. This exhibition, bringing together as it does, contemporary work of excellence from all parts of the world, could not be more propitious. The Victoria and Albert Museum is the right venue and the Metalwork Department is to be congratulated on its perfect timing and extraordinary foresight.

Victor Margrie
Director of the Crafts Council

On Ironwork

The blacksmith works with a very ancient material, whose immense practical usefulness doubtless inspired the classical myth of Vulcan, the blacksmith-god who forged iron. More recently however iron has attracted the attention of artist-craftsmen, and has thus also become a medium for sculpture and the decorative arts.

Design has always been the source of inspiration for artist-blacksmiths, the means whereby the material is translated into an object by way of an intimate knowledge of the metal and its technology. Thus for today's blacksmith design is partly a scientific investigation, partly the expression of an idea which requires a profound insight into the decorative aspects of ironworking. This need not however preclude today's technological innovations; I myself forge iron with a power-hammer, solder it electrically and cut it with oxymethalene gas, as well as using traditional methods of forging. This entails experimentation with new forms, forms that are an expression of the spirit of the age, for the past can only have the role of mentor. The pedestrian reproduction of the images of yesterday is an unworthy task — unless specifically intended as restoration — itself a work of reintegration. Surely any alert and receptive artist looking about at the panoply of modern styles can find one which is the ideal for what he wishes to communicate?

In the past I have experimented with figurative and monumental sculpture but I am primarily interested at present in how to project form into space in the urban environment. This means in practice environmental sculpture, for example, *The Cathedral*, at Belluno, the gateway to the Terraferma at Mestre, or the memorial to Lidice at Prague. The artists who have influenced me are Mazzucotelli, with his extraordinary ability to synthesize idea and form; Arturo Martini, a great innovator and experimenter; and Brancusi, for his concentration on the problem of sculptural space.

In 1967 I founded a training school for artist-blacksmiths: the Accademia del Ferro at Marocco di Treviso. This has proved very successful, and its pupils, drawn from all over the world, have amply demonstrated the benefits of a rigorous apprenticeship combined with the study of the history of iron, involving an awareness of artistic styles, and of the uses of iron in sculpture and in architecture.

The craft of blacksmithing has enormous potential for modern design, as witnessed by the achievements of famous blacksmiths of the recent past as well as of the present. However, its future still gives cause for concern, for reasons both economic and cultural. This ancient craft, in the past so prolific of masterpieces, seems today in danger of faltering, largely because of a general lack of sensitivity to its artistic possibilities, and to the specific technical problems posed by iron.

(translated from the Italian)

Antonio Benetton

Illustration: Garden with giant iron sculptures made by Antonio Benetton.

Forged Ironwork today

Five years ago, this exhibition would have been inconceivable. In the first place, there was in Britain at that time almost no knowledge of, or contact with, the work of blacksmiths abroad. Secondly, most blacksmiths in Britain produced work that was derivative in design — they looked to seventeenth and eighteenth-century models, attracted by their elegance and by the high level of manual skill required to make them. Smiths were then an extraordinarily conservative breed. Thus, by the 1970s, in spite of the efforts of the Council for Small Industries in Rural Areas (Co SIRA) to maintain the craft's standards by offering short courses for apprentices and working craftsmen, blacksmithing in Britain had reached a low ebb. The blacksmiths themselves were isolated, not only geographically from each other, but from opportunities to develop their design thinking in, for example, art college courses; from architects and other patrons; from contemporary developments in visual arts and crafts in this country and abroad. In addition, forgework had largely disappeared from the curriculum of schools and teacher-training institutions. The craft was static.

It was also under threat. Unlike the farrier, whose specific skill — the shoeing of horses — has survived many vicissitudes, the ornamental smith has been the victim of large-scale industrial and social changes, starting even before the introduction in the eighteenth century of cast ironwork that imitated the forms of forged iron. In the twentieth century, architural styles and building methods have changed so radically that there is now little demand for ornamental ironwork; even where a demand exists, the smith must compete with the manufacturers of mass-produced components.

Despite all this, the craft has survived. Blacksmiths have continued to produce traditional-style ornamental gates and railings. Much restoration work has been done, and small-scale domestic items such as firegrates, screens, pokers have been made that often aptly reconcile function with the decorative features attendant in the making process. But it recently became clear that some fundamental change was urgently needed if blacksmithing was to survive into the twenty-first century.

This exhibition demonstrates that changes have indeed taken place. How did they come about? In 1977 Ivan Smith, a passionate advocate for his craft, put the blacksmiths' dilemma to the Crafts Council in eloquent terms, stressing the enormous potential of this difficult craft, and the need for a new imaginative breakthrough. A small exploratory committee was set up to review the problems; its members were Ivan Smith, Richard Quinnell (Managing Director of R. Quinnell Ltd.), Claude Blair (Keeper of Metalwork at the V & A), Neil Cossons (Director of Ironbridge Gorge Museum), Victor Margrie (Director of the Crafts Council) and myself, as its secretary. From that moment, there was a dramatic increase in activity. Contacts were made abroad and in 1978, with the help of a Churchill Fellowship and the British Council, Richard Quinnell and I visited 30 forges in Germany, Austria, Switzerland, Italy and France. Richard Quinnell had already visited American blacksmiths, at the invitation of the Artist Blacksmiths' Association of North America (ABANA), and this experience led to the formation of the British Artist Blacksmiths' Association (BABA) also in 1978. In 1979 the Crafts Council organised a small-scale International Experimental Workshop, and in 1980 a major International Conference at Hereford, attended by 150 smiths from all parts of the world, with particularly strong representation from the USA and the German-speaking countries.

These events attracted the attention of smiths who were already experimenting with iron, attempting to give it new forms appropriate to the tastes and attitudes of our own time. The breakthrough came when these smiths met artist-craftsmen from abroad who designed and made their own work with confidence and flair, deftly using the whole range of hand techniques in combination with the newer, semi-industrial technology of power-hammer, gas and arc welder, and oxyacetylene torch. These foreign craftsmen had had the benefit of a much broader training and the example of the outstanding work being produced in their own countries. In their hands, iron became plastic, three-dimensional and full of potential for subtle sculptural form, whilst its surface became alive with textures and colours resulting from the heating, hammering and cutting processes. They could forge massive sections under the power-hammer and cut thick plate with the oxyacetylene torch — but also, with a few blows of the hand-hammer, forge delicate leaves that had life in them. They had escaped from the tyranny of outdated styles.

From here onwards I shall describe the work and the approach of some of the craftsmen who have had a particular impact on blacksmithing today, largely because of the lectures and demonstration they gave at the 1980 Hereford Conference.

Illustration: Fritz Kühn Screen, 1958, Mild steel.

Germany and Italy had taken the lead in twentieth century forged ironwork. The late *Fritz Kühn*, whose career spanned 30 years, began by finding new and creative ways of applying the traditional techniques of the craft. Later he began his 'form experiments': alongside the observations he recorded in drawings and photography, and he used the electron microscope to discover new structures in nature, which he incorporated into his work. He also etched, coloured and flashed the surface of the iron with other metals: 'Because I can see how the steel is changed with additions of tungsten, chrome, nickel, molybdenum, carbon, how the structure is altered by bending, heating, quenching and tempering, I am filled with the desire to bring this inner language of the metal, which we work every day, to the surface and to give it visible form'[1] Kühn was also a gifted writer and communicator; he published 12 books, lectured and made teaching films.

The rich potential of Kühn's technique is illustrated by exhibit No.76, *Drei Bunde* (three bands); his attention to surface texture by exhibits 73 and 75, *Zinnie* (Zinnia) and *Erstarrte Bewegung* (frozen motion). He was also interested in letter-forms, which he used to great effect on the entrance for the Berlin City library; see exhibit 74. He liked to work on an architectural scale, and one of his greatest achievements was his screen for the East German pavilion at the 1958 World Exhibition in Brussels, now on permanent exhibition on the island of Lindau, West Germany; photograph on page 11.

His son *Achim Kühn*, who trained as an architect, took over the running of the Berlin workshop when his father died in 1967. Achim's primary concern is to 'build with metal'[2] – rather than merely add it as a decorative element – whether the work is part of a building, such as exhibit 71, *Schwingender Stahl* (swinging steel), or whether it is free-standing, like the sculptures *Steel Sculpture* exhibit 73 and *Verdrehung* (Torsion) exhibit 72. At the same time, his work is intended to arrest the viewer and make him reflect about himself and his times.

Inspired by men such as Fritz Kühn, and trained in the excellent schools that existed in Munich, Stuttgart and Aachen, blacksmiths throughout the German-speaking world are now producing new work of high quality. *Manfred Bredohl*, one of Ulrich's students, is well-known for the bold way he uses the power hammer to produce the repeated decorative motifs of his railings, grilles and gates.

Herman Gradinger (page 32) also shapes decorative elements directly under the power-hammer, in combination with cutting and arc welding, methods that have become characteristic of much German ironwork today. Gradinger has developed a mature personal style that is characterised by sound overall proportions combined with skill and expressiveness in the forging.

Paul Zimmermann's (page 57) work is more obviously 'organic' in feeling, though he uses the same techniques. He is fond of curves and pays great attention to the hammered and cut edges of his work (*see* his *Candleholder* exhibit 148) and to the richness of the hammered surfaces (*see* his *Candleholder* exhibit 149).

Manfred and German Bergmeister (page 27) run the largest workshop in West Germany that produces work of an individual style; they employ 20 craftsmen. The Bergmeisters' architectural ironwork is characterised by its logical construction and its precise and confident workmanship; see exhibit 15, which was also shown at the most recent international exhibition of ironwork in Lindau. Much of the Bergmeisters' exterior work is made of an alloy known as 'forging bronze', which does not rust.

Another, more personal aspect of Manfred Bergmeister's work can be seen in his grave-crosses (see exhibit 16) and in his sculptures, which exploit the resistance of the material as it is being worked.

The harmonious domestic items of the Czech *Jan Dudesek* (page 31) who now works in Switzerland show a fine sense of line and attention to technical detail; his barbecue and poker set were seen at Lindau. In stark contrast are the disquieting 'machine-being' sculptures of the Austrian *Walfrid Huber*; and a photograph of them is included in the exhibition (no.64).

The Czech smith, *Alfred Habermann* (page 33) began by restoring Czech ironwork of all periods. This exploration of the material led him to work with Professor Antonio Benetton at his International Academy of Iron (see below). Habermann is a highly-skilled craftsman, and one of his most successful pieces is a sundial shown at the Lindau exhibition in 1980. Since then, he has spent a month at the Dyfed College of Art in Wales, working on a commission with the Czech sculptor Vaclav Jaros.

---

1 'Forging Iron' Conference Papers: Notes on the work of Fritz Kuhn and Achim Kuhn 1980 p.3.   2 Ibid p.6.

The other main source of inspiration is an Italian, *Professor Antonio Benetton*, who has contributed an essay to this catalogue (page 8). After an initial technical and craft training and some years studying sculpture, Toni Benetton has spent his long life — he was born in 1910 — working with his favourite material, iron. His researches have passed through many phases, and his current preoccupation is with the projection of space in urban settings. He exerts his influence both through his own work in Italy and through the International Academy of Iron which he set up, and still runs, at his workshop in Marocco, near Treviso. The development of his work can clearly be seen in the magnificent permanent exhibition in his own gallery and park; exhibit 10 has been lent from that display. His work has appeared in limited editions that have circulated within Italy, and on film; we hope to show some of these films during the run of the exhibition in order to do full justice to a life spent in creative search. Toni Benetton was guest of honour at the Crafts Council's International Conference.

His son *Simon Benetton* demonstrated the technique of cutting plate with the oxyacetylene torch at the Council's Experimental Workshop in 1979.

The gifted French iron sculptor *Serge Marchal* (page 45) from Nimes made an enormous impact at the 1979 experimental workshop and at the Hereford Conference. He is a member of the French trade training association, the Association Ouvrière des Compagnons du Devoir, and for his masterpiece made a light-sculpture that filled the stairwell from floor to roof in the training centre in Nimes. He is concerned with expressing the forces of nature and is represented in this exhibition by a sculpture called *Wind*.

Daniel Souriou taught Serge Marchal. His own work is a sensitive exploration of forged sculpture on a fine scale.

The revival of interest in blacksmithing in the USA has been quite remarkable: the Artist Blacksmiths' Association of North America (ABANA), founded in 1973 with 27 members 'to preserve a dying craft', now has a membership of 1,500.[3] This revival is increasingly influencing Europe. Meetings that bring together blacksmiths from both sides of the Atlantic can therefore be of great mutual benefit, as demonstrated at the Hereford conference. The American influence has also been spread through European participation in ABANA's own conference in the USA, and through the Association's excellent journal *The Anvil's Ring*. It is impossible in so short an essay to do more than mention the work of a few smiths that made a particular impression on the international gathering; a much fuller picture can be gained from Dona Meilach's recent book *Decorative and Sculptural Ironwork* (see bibliography). The Hereford Conference saw elegant sleds and Damascus steel knives (exhibits 131 and 132) from *Jim Wallace*; well-made architectural ironwork that combined inventiveness with a high standard of technique from *Eric Moebius* and *Bruce Le Page*; gates and railings in a highly accomplished personal style (exhibits 93 to 97) from the jeweller turned blacksmith *Albert Paley*.

Before discussing the work of smiths in Britain, I should mention that Western influence has recently spread to Japan. Although their metalworking skills traditionally lie in sword-making, armour and cast ironwork, Japanese craftsmen have now begun to make forged ironwork in the European tradition. This exhibition therefore shows the beginnings of a new craft in Japan: the making of completely different types of object that are nevertheless permeated with Japanese experience and taste. *Minamizawa's* work (exhibits 87 and 88) shows the Japanese influence more strongly than that of *Takayoshi Komine* (exhibits 68 to 70) who has spent some time working with smiths in Germany.

Blacksmithing in Britain has undergone a dramatic change in the past few years, as smiths have begun to develop their own personal styles or 'hand writing', as Hermann Gradinger calls it.

Anthony Robinson has been experimenting for many years, and recently his work has come to fruition with the designs for a magnificent pair of double gates for the mediaeval Great Hall of Winchester Castle: see drawing in exhibition (no. 155). These gates, which commemorate the Royal Wedding, are to be forged in stainless steel and will be completed in July 1982, the first anniversary of the wedding.

James Horrobin won the limited design competition for a pair of gates for the V & A's own Ironwork Galleries. Son of a blacksmith, he is steeped in the traditional techniques, and in his most recent work is exploring ways of using these afresh.

---

3 See Dimitri Gerakaris, 'International Ironwork', *Crafts* no.53, November-December 1981, pp.41-42.

A yet further competition for a pair of gates, for the new Treasury in the crypt of St Paul's Cathedral, was won by *Alan Evans*. His design (see photograph 41) was inspired by the curves of the vaulted ceiling;[4] the main bows of the gates were cut out from a template and then forged.

Stuart Hill is noted for his inventive use of a variety of metalworking techniques beside forging, Firebasket (exhibit 50) is an example of the use of cut plate. Hill is currently preoccupied with large-scale architectural metalwork that creates patterns of light and shadow by means of distortion of bars. His 'metamorphosis table', which won him the Organisers' Prize at Lindau and is now in the V&A's permanent collection, demonstrates his forging skills — the frogs are made from one piece of iron. By contrast, the majority of *Giuseppe Lund's* work — such as his spiral staircase (exhibit 83) — is forged under the power hammer and makes dramatic use of the plastic quality of the metal.

This exhibition also shows some unexpected ways in which forged ironwork can be used: for a car park barrier (by Ronald Eastman), for a chair (by Kauko Moisio), for jewellery (by David Poston, Ruth Stourton, Alison Varley, David Watkins and others). Both mild and stainless steel are becoming increasingly popular with jewellers, and the standard of design and craftsmanship they demonstrate is exceptionally high.

The aim of this exhibition is to show a body of experimental work of high quality to a public that has never before had this opportunity. Clearly ironwork has enormous potential in the hands of craftsmen or women with imagination and skill. What the blacksmiths of all countries need is the chance to develop that potential through a dialogue, whether it is with the informed architect or designer, or with the interested layman. There is a renewed interest in the decoration of buildings, so the climate is favourable. For his part, the blacksmith must take advantage of the entire range of techniques now available to him and make them serve his imagination. If his taste is sure, the technique he uses will be right for the job in hand. If smiths begin to use tradition as a safety-rail, a reference point, but remove the dust from it to make it more lively and natural — as Serge Marchal recommended at the International Conference — who can predict the works that will emerge?[5]

Caroline Pearce-Higgins

4 *Crafts* no. 54, January/February 1982, pp.45-49.   5 'Forging Iron' Conference Papers, 1980. Notes on Tradition by Serge Marchal.

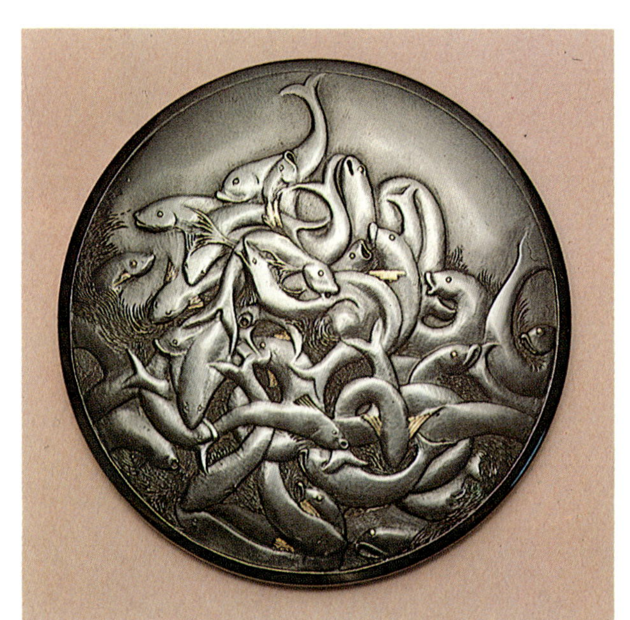

During this century, blacksmithing has undergone a significant change, from a period of vigorous activity and high quality in Art Nouveau and Art Deco, between c. 1890 and 1939, through a decline and change of emphasis during the Second World War and its aftermath, to its present international resurgence.

The most fundamental change in twentieth century blacksmithing has been in the role of the blacksmith himself. From a position, in many cases, of subservience to the architect, in which the blacksmith acted as artisan-craftsman, the smith's artistic autonomy is beginning to be re-established. This renewal of independence, in terms of innovatory design, is a marked feature of the best recent developments in the craft, and demonstrates the move away, by certain blacksmiths, from the traditional 18th century concept of scrollwork. The identification of the 'artist blacksmith' as a distinct entity has also confirmed the independence of the craft from farriery.

The period of Art Nouveau, between c. 1890 and 1914, witnessed extensive and highly imaginative uses of wrought ironwork, the organic forms of much Art Nouveau architecture providing a receptive setting for its embellishment. Frequently, such fittings were designed by the architect himself, employing the blacksmith as craftsman only, rather than commissioning independent designs. Such an approach was adopted by Charles Rennie Mackintosh, in the ironwork of Glasgow School of Art, executed between 1899 and 1909, by Messrs. George Adam and Son, and R. Smith and Co. (ill. 1). The strength of Mackintosh's work lies both in its originality, but an originality which still stems from tradition, and in his direct supervision of the blacksmiths during the process of manufacture. This is most apparent in the ends of the T-section girders supporting the roof of the basement sculpture studios, where these project deliberately from the wall surface (ill. 2).[1]

The Turin exhibition of 1902 included amongst Mackintosh's fellow participants the Milanese blacksmith Alessandro Mazzucotelli (1865-1938). An outstanding master of Art Nouveau ironwork, Mazzucotelli had a highly successful business, working in collaboration with such architects as Sommaruga, and on his own design initiative, to create predominantly architectural fittings, which vary in character from foliate imagery, (ill. 3) to a more abstract geometric manner,

---

1 H. Jefferson Barnes, former Director of Glasgow School of Art, has maintained that the splitting and coiling of the ends by the blacksmiths concerned caused one of the two stoppages on the building, such was the apparent impossibility of the task.

recalling parallels with the Secessionist ironwork of Darmstadt, and
Otto Wagner's ironwork for the Vienna subway. The vigour of
Mazzucotelli's work, coupled with its technical virtuosity, is highly
impressive. Such achievements depend for their realization on a
healthy economic climate: in a number of cases, Mazzucotelli's
clients were captains of the Lombardy textile industry, for which he
also designed. Both this versatility, and his dependence on
patronage, invites comparison with Mackintosh.

Mazzucotelli's achievements have been widely recognised; he won
awards at the Milan exhibition of 1906, the Brussels exhibition of
1910, and the Paris exhibition of 1925. The imagination and
strength of his work suggests comparisons also with the ironwork of
Antonio Gaudi, but unlike the latter, Mazzucotelli acted as both
designer and craftsman, rather than delegating the execution of his
work to a different firm.

The effect of presence conveyed by Mazzucotelli's ironwork has a
more dynamic relationship to its architectural setting than much Art
Deco work, where the greater emphasis on geometry and two
dimensionality creates a tighter sense of control. Nonetheless,
ironwork was in notable evidence at the Paris 1925 *Exposition des
Arts Decoratifs et Modernes*.[2] Here, too, the extent of commercial
patronage was significant. One major French smith who benefitted
thus was Edgar Brandt (1880-1960), whose commissions included
metalwork for Selfridges, the London department store. Executed
between 1922 and 1928, his lift-cage panels for them combined
wrought iron and beaten tin plate (V&A Circ. 719-1971; ill. 4).

A direct contemporary of Brandt's was Samuel Yellin (1885-1940),
an outstandingly successful American smith. Born in Poland, Yellin
began his training at the age of seven in a Russian forge, followed by
similar experience in Belgium and England. The skills he acquired
varied widely and he made objects ranging from nails and armour, to
Gothic- and Renaissance-style ironwork. Arriving in Philadelphia in
1906, he built up his enterprise in the 1920s to one of the largest
ever blacksmithing studios, employing over three hundred men, many
of them immigrants who were already experienced smiths. The
commercial extent and success of Yellin's business depended on his
ability to design and custom-build large commissions for specific
clients and architects, including much of the ironwork for Washington
Cathedral.[3]

---

2 Our knowledge of Art Deco ironwork depends to a fair degree on the publications of H. Clouzot
   who, in addition to his study of ironwork at the 1925 Paris exhibition, published in 1926 a
   companion volume, *La Ferronerie Moderne*.

3 The traditionalism of Yellin's prowess has been commemorated by his son, Harvey Yellin, in a
   private museum in Philadelphia, which includes actual examples of all Yellin's major

2 Charles Rennie Mackintosh, detail of T-girder, split and forged into a sculptural form, supporting one of the main roof timbers in the basement sculpture studios, Glasgow School of Art, c. 1908.

Photo credit: Glasgow School of Art.

3 Alessandro Mazzucotelli, detail of wrought ironwork from the exterior of the Villa Enrico Ottolini, Busto Arsizio (Varese), Italy, built between 1900 and 1903 (now a school). Mazzucotelli's ironwork for this commission was extensive, including gates, grilles, railings, indoor and exterior lamps. Considered one of his masterpieces, this ensemble makes particularly striking use of vegetal and animal imagery.

Photo Credit: Arno Hammacher, Milan.

4 Edgar Brandt, lift-cage panel, wrought iron and beaten plate, formerly part of the fittings of Selfridges Ltd, Oxford Street, London. 1922-1928. Victoria & Albert Museum, Circ. 719-1971. The central octagon is a characteristic iconographic motif of 1920s decoration, frequently used at the Paris exhibition of 1925, where Brandt was also a prominent participant.

Photo credit: Crown copyright.

---

commissions. The first major retrospective exhibition of Yellin's work will tour the USA in 1982-3; information from Jack Andrew, Paoli, Pa.

4 See the catalogue of the recent Arts Council exhibition, *Sir Edwin Lutyens*, Hayward Gallery, London, 1981-2, for a fuller account of this collaboration.

In Britain, blacksmithing during the 1920s and 1930s was heavily dominated by tradition. This combination of historicism with technical competence has been perpetuated until the 1950s and beyond, its persistence deriving from the essential conservatism of both smith and client, the popularity and perpetuation of neo-Georgian architecture and, by contrast, the plainer requirements of the Modern Movement in architecture, which eschewed any floridity in ornament, in favour of a purist aesthetic.

Symptomatic of the traditionalist approach were the designs of John Seymour Lindsay (1882-1966). During the 1930s, working as a designer in collaboration with a Suffolk blacksmith, he produced ironwork which included, for Sir Herbert Baker, fittings in the Bank of England (1921-37), and, for Baker and Sir Edwin Lutyens, light-fittings and ironwork in the Government buildings, New Delhi.[4]

One further factor affecting the continuing traditionalism of much twentieth century British blacksmithing has been the educational role played by the Council for Small Industries in Rural Areas (CoSIRA). Its training courses and handbooks, supervised for many years by Zanni and then by Tommy Tucker, have ensured the induction of young blacksmithing apprentices to the vocabulary of traditional methods and design, coupled with sound craftsmanship.

More modern educational approaches, in design terms, were adopted by the late Fritz Kuhn (1910-1967), and by Toni Benetton (b.1910), both of whom are represented in this exhibition. Kuhn's family background in metalwork, and his conventional apprenticeship ensured his technical mastery, from which he developed an ability to design work of outstanding quality. This was widely recognised by, for example, his inclusion in the Brussels World Fair of 1958, and by his one-man exhibition at the Musée des Arts Decoratifs, Paris in 1969.

In contrast to the fundamentally traditional training of Fritz Kühn, Toni Benetton, regarded by many as the doyen of Italian blacksmiths today, began his training in sculpture — a medium with which he still identifies.

The Second World War had a widespread effect on blacksmithing. Englishmen such as Norman Bucknell, of Bisley, Gloucestershire, who trained with his father, Alfred, the designer Ernest Gimson's blacksmith, were directed during the war from smithing into engineering. Conversely, Reg Butler, renowned for his forged iron, abstract, spiky sculptures, learnt his skills as a smith by working in that capacity during wartime. Bucknell chose to return to blacksmithing, producing high quality domestic ironwork to Gimson's designs, remaining essentially traditional in character and appearance. Butler's experimental innovation has been recognised by a source of inspiration among certain smiths working today.

Such exchanges of experience accentuate the evolving character of present-day blacksmithing from its traditional inheritance of forged scrollwork. As indicated previously, blacksmiths from the 1950s onwards have, in a number of cases, reassserted their artistic and design autonomy, developing the ability to initiate their own designs, whilst continuing to work in close collaboration with commissioning architects and clients. Fundamental to their successful re-establishment has been sufficient patronage. This is particularly evident in West Germany, where, post-war, the German state has allocated 10% of all income tax to the church, thus ensuring the ready availability of funds for the rebuilding and embellishment of this important resource for ironwork. Such financial investment has been matched by similarly generous patronage by the State. This, with the vigorous continuance of the craft apprenticeship system explains in large part Germany's importance in contemporary forged ironwork.

In America, as in Britain, the background of smiths working today is a varied one. In a number of cases — e.g. Brent Kington and Albert Paley — the interest in forged large-scale metalwork has emerged from a background of training as a jeweller. It is in post-World War II American jewellery that the use of mixed and non-precious metals has been most evident. The recently depressed state of the economy, together with the increased price of gold and silver have combined to stimulate American and British jewellers, amongst others, to work in other media. Such versatility in the use of materials and techniques has produced a range of interesting results, some of which are illustrated in this exhibition. Both in jewellery and in larger-scale domestic and architectural ironwork, the uses of forged ironwork and mild steel which have been developed since the late 1960s offer a variety of approaches, the stimulus of recent work suggesting a healthy promise for the future.

Dorothy Bosomworth

Iron: the metal and the smiths

Iron is one of the most abundant of elements, accounting for about 35% of the earth's weight, while the earth's core is itself molten iron. In its pure form it is a ductile, malleable, silvery metal, strong, but prone to corrosion. Metallic iron is rare in nature, and the greater part of it occurs in the form of meteorites from outer space. It is far more commonly found in the reddish earths known as *iron ore*, from which the metal can only be extracted by applying intense heat. By about 3500 BC man had mastered the technique of 'roasting' (diffusion reduction) the ore with charcoal at a temperature of about 1200°C. This produced a 'bloom' or lump of iron mixed with impurities, which could be removed by hand hammering. The Iron Age, when iron objects — tools and weapons — first came into common use can only be said to have begun in about 1500 BC, apparently in the Middle East; it spread slowly through the known world only reaching the British Isles in about the 5th century BC.

The addition of 0.3 to 2.2 percent carbon to iron converts it into *steel*. If the carbon content is further increased to 2.2 to 5 percent it becomes *cast* or *pig iron* which is very hard and brittle and will shatter if *forged* (hammered) or rolled; it is therefore useless to the smith. Cast iron can only be shaped by remelting and casting into moulds; it has been and remains a valuable material for certain engineering and ornamental purposes. Crucially however it is the basic metal from which wrought iron and steel can be produced after further processing.

The types of iron most commonly used by blacksmiths are *wrought iron* and *mild steel*. *Wrought iron* is a fairly pure form of the metal containing threads of glassy *slag* (waste material, mainly silicates) absorbed during the refining process, and is now made by hand-stirring (*puddling*) moulten pig iron so as to burn out the dissolved carbon. The solidified lumps are forged into ingots with a power-hammer, then rolled into bars. Wrought iron is tough, fairly soft, and has a woody grain that can be seen when a bar is etched with acid. However, because its manufacture is very labour-intensive, little is now made in the developed countries.

Most blacksmiths now use *mild steel*, a less pure from of iron, containing 0.15-0.25 percent carbon that is more uniform in structure without the pronounced grain of wrought iron. Mild steel is widely used for engineering purposes: the manufacture of ships, cars, bridges, the structure of buildings, etc. It is made in bulk from pig iron, by a process that yields hundreds of tonnes at a time; by contrast, the best a wrought iron puddler can manage are 50-kilogramme lumps. A blacksmith can nowadays buy mild steel, in a wide variety of ready-formed solid and hollow sections: bars, rod, strips, angles, tubes, I- and H girders, etc.

Wrought iron and mild steel are, in practice, both referred to by blacksmiths simply as 'iron'. They look similar — both are silvery when freshly cut, but become blue-black with oxide after forging, and red with rust when exposed to damp air and are equally prone to corrosion. For certain smithing operations, each has certain advantages over the other, but the overall differences are academic.

For blacksmiths, the most valuable property of iron is that, when red-hot, it softens almost to the consistency of plasticine. In this state it can be freely shaped: hammered on the anvil, bent, flattened, split, cut, twisted and indented. Iron is unusual among metals in that two pieces can be welded to each other perfectly if hammered together when hot.

In most climates, iron begins to *oxidise* (rust) as soon as it is smelted from its ore. Most blacksmiths inhibit this process by coating the metal with a layer of zinc, aluminium or paint, whilst a few prefer to leave the natural surface.

Equipment and Techniques

The working of iron requires equipment for various processes: the initial preparation of the bar or sheet metal; heating, forging and cutting it into shape when hot; and welding, filing, grinding, drilling and finishing it when cold. The basic techniques, and the basic functions of the equipment used, are age-old, but modern technology — especially the development of the power-hammer, the portable grinder, the arc welder, and the oxyacetylene welder and cutter — has given the blacksmith of today the ability to work more quickly and easily in heavy metal. He is thus able to include in his repertoire effects that are new, or that were formerly only possible with much labour; this has greatly influenced design.

Basic forge equipment

The most important pieces of equipment in a blacksmith's forge are:

The Anvil. The standard anvil is mounted upon a block of wood that serves as a shock absorber, and consists of a block of iron or steel with a flat, polished working surface and a projecting horn at one or both ends. Let into the work surface is a circular *pritchel-hole* (or punching-hole) and a rectangular *hardie-hole* (or tool-hole). The pritchel-hole is merely an aperture that allows a punch to be driven through work supported on the face of the anvil. The hardie-hole serves to secure fixed anvil tools, of which the most common are: *stakes*, miniature anvils of various forms suitable for producing special shapes in the metal; the *hardie*, a wedge-shaped chisel used for splitting hot metal or for cutting off lengths; *swages*, simple dies having an upper and lower part and used for finishing metal rods and finials in convex shapes. The two holes can be used to hold tools improvised for special purposes, and also devices for securing the work at times when the smith needs to use both hands. A tub or trough of water for cooling the iron is usually placed near the anvil.

The Bench and Vice. The bench is of normal form, often metal-topped, and is used for laying out work and for keeping tools close to hand. The vice, bolted to the bench and the floor, is a robust clamp used to hold the work-piece securely for both hot and cold working.

Chisels (both hot and cold), some fitted with a wooden handle or rod, are used for cutting.

Drifts, tapered steel rods that are driven through holes made with punches to enlarge and shape them, or to split the metal.

Forge Hearth. The fire in which the metal is heated before it is worked. Though gas-fire hearths are available, most smiths prefer the traditional type fuelled with coke or coal (or, less commonly nowadays, charcoal). The heat of the fire is controlled by hand-operated bellows or by a centrifugal blower, usually electric-powered.

Fullers, round-nosed chisels for making grooves.

Hand-hammers. Many different weights, with a wide variety of head-shapes, are used for working the metal, usually when it is hot.

Punches for making and clearing holes.

Tongs of different shapes and sizes for holding and manipulating the hot metal.

Cutting, drilling and abrading equipment

In addition to the traditional *hacksaw* and *hand-shears* for cutting, *hand-drill* for making holes, and the *hand-file* for smoothing and shaping, the following power tools may be used: *abrasive cutter* with carborundum wheel, for heavy-duty cutting; *band-saw* for cutting-off and shaping; *circular saw* for cutting-off; *drill* for making holes; *ironworker* for cutting-off, shearing, notching and punching holes. The oxyacetylene cutter, which has a high-temperature flame produced by burning a mixture of oxygen and acetylene under pressure, burns the steel or iron locally and enables the smith to cut substantial thicknesses very quickly; it also produces decorative textures and effects not obtainable by any other means. Though long employed in heavy industry, the oxyacetylene cutter has only recently come into general use among artist-blacksmiths.

The portable *grinder and sander*, which uses abrasive wheels for metal removal and surface smoothing, can perform the functions of files and emery paper at very much greater speeds.

Finishing

Traditionally, iron was finished by painting it to prevent rust. Nowadays, since buildings are generally drier, internal ironwork is often left with its natural finish, protected only by a coat of transparent lacquer or wax. The metal is usually pickled in acid to remove oxide scales and rust left by the forge, and then burnished. But some smiths leave the surface rough from the forge, even to the extent of allowing it to continue rusting. Other finishes, both protective and decorative, include: *electro-plating* with a thin film of copper, nickel, chromium or zinc; *galvanizing* by dipping in molten zinc, which, though a particularly effective rust protector, is liable to clog detail and spoil surface texture; *flame-metallization* by spraying with molten metal, usually zinc or aluminium, which confers improved rust-resistance with minimum loss of detail. Modern paints, stove enamels and plastic coatings also offer a wide range of decorative effects combined with protection from the atmosphere.

Mechanical forging and forming equipment

Power hammer. Although water- and steam-powered hammers have for centuries been used in heavy forging, only in recent years have compact precision power-hammers become generally available. They have increased the quantity and size of work that a blacksmith can produce single-handed, while their flexibility, the result of interchangeable top and bottom dies (in effect, hammers and anvils), and their capacity to work hot iron as if it were plasticine, has had a major influence on design. Smiths are now able to produce a freedom of final effect almost unobtainable by traditional methods.

Press. Some blacksmiths are now using the *fly-press*, which, by means of a screw and weight, enables single precise forming operations to be carried out, cold or hot, with dies. The more powerful *hydraulic press* can be used for the same purpose.

Welding and joining

The traditional method of welding two pieces of iron and steel is to heat them to a high temperature in the forge and then hammer them on the anvil until they fuse together. But this process is only possible with work that can be placed bodily in the fire. The oxyacetylene flame and the electric arc-welder, both of which can melt steel, are now widely used instead, since they make *direct-fusion welding* possible; the source of heat can be taken to the work, thus enabling the construction of objects that would not fit into the fire. This has greatly increased the range of designs available to the smith. MIG (Metal Inert Gas) welding is an even more precise method.

Other joining methods used by blacksmiths include: riveting, bolting, screwing, collaring (small metal collars encircling the parts to be joined together) and mortising, as in carpentry.

Claude Blair and Richard Quinnell

Catalogue

(Entries under the headings **Exhibitions**, **Public Collections** and **Publications** are selective)
Asterisk denotes illustrated in catalogue.

Malcolm Appleby

Crathes Station, Banchory, Kincardineshire, Scotland

1946	born in Beckenham, Kent
1961-63	Beckenham School of Art, Ravensbourne; did some engraving
1963-65	Central School of Arts and Crafts
1965-66	Sir John Cass College
1966-68	Royal College of Art; part time apprenticeship to John Wilkes, gunsmiths of Beak Street, London. At present: visiting lecturer, Royal College of Art

Exhibitions

1973	*The Craftsman's Art* V&A and Crafts Council
1977	*Explosion; talent today* Goldsmiths' Hall, London
1977	*Treasures of London* Vancouver and Montreal, Canada
1982	*The Maker's Eye* Crafts Council

Public Collections

Crafts Council, Goldsmiths' Hall, V&A

Publications

The ring from antiquity to the 20th century — B. Cartlidge, J. Cherry, C. Gere, A. Ward (Fribourg and London 1981)

Exhibits

1* Woodcock gun 1981
12-bore side lock ejector shotgun. Walnut and steel; the gun by John Wilkes, Chilton locks and engraving designed and executed by Malcolm Appelby. Approx 119cm long x 18cm wide. Colln. Malcolm Appleby

2 Hawk ring 1967-1968
Mild steel, inlaid with gold and silver. Max diam 3.8cm. Colln. Malcolm Appleby

3 Ring 1981
Iron (from gun barrel section), inlaid with gold, Diam: 2.2cm. Colln. Malcolm Appleby

4* Duck Bangle 1975
Iron (burnished), and 24 ct. gold. Diam: 6.8cm. Private Colln.

5 Ring 1981
Iron (from gun barrel section) inlaid with gold and silver. Diam: 2.1cm. Colln. Malcolm Appleby

6* Torc 1981
Iron inlaid with 24 ct. gold. Approx diam. 13cm. Private Colln.

7* Bangle 1979
Iron inlaid with 24 ct. Approx diam. 7cm. Private Colln.

8 Ring 1981
Iron (from gun barrel section) engraved and inlaid with 24 ct. gold lined in silver. 1cm wide x 2.8cm diam. Colln. Malcolm Appleby

Phillip Baldwin

206

516E Loren, Springfield, MO 65807, USA

1953	born in New York City, USA
1967	first interest in blacksmithing
1976	BA degree
1977	worked for Dynell Electronics Corp Solid Photography Div, Melville, NY as sculptor and technical assistant
1977-79	studied metalworking at Southern Illinois University at Carbondale. MA 1979
1978	taught blacksmithing at Carbondale
1978-79	research into Japanese *mokume* and granulation
1978	museum merit award for Jewellery, Evansville Museum of Arts and Sciences, Evansville, Ind.
1981	taught non-ferrous metal forging at Oregon School of Arts and Crafts, Portland, Oregon
1973-74, 1976	periods working at sculpture foundry of Joel Meisner & Co as wax-chaser, bronze-chaser, heliarc welder
1979	first prize in metals at Missisippi River Craft Show Brooks Memorial Art Gallery, Memphis, Tenn.

Antonio Benetton

Exhibitions

1977   *Art of the Blacksmith* Trenton State College, NJ

1979   *Mid-States Craft Exhibition* Evansville Museum of Arts and Sciences
House Jewelry National Ornamental Metals Museum Memphis, Tenn.
Missisippi Rivercraft Show Brooks Memorial Gallery, Memphis Tenn.

1980   *Metalsmithing 1980*. Sesnon Art Galleries, Univ of California. California, Santa Cruz, CA

Publications

Anvil's Ring vol 9 nos. 1,2
American Craft vol 41, no 3

Public Collections

National Ornamental Metals Museum, Memphis, Tenn. Carbondale University Museum & Art Galleries, Oregon School of Arts & Crafts

Exhibit

9* Knife 'Nightfighter III' 1978

Wood and mild steel, forged, filed, stoned, inlaid with silver. 11.5 x 51cm long x 2.5cm wide. Colln. P. Baldwin

207

Via Marignana 112, 31021 Mogliana-Veneto-Treviso, Italy

1910   born in Treviso, Italy

1928   attended a conference in Milan on 'L'Arte del Ferro' at which he met Mazzucotelli, Carlo Rizzarda, Umberto Bellotto and Calligari

1933-37   taught at the Scuola Tecnica Industriale in Treviso

1938-42   studied sculpture under Arturo Martini at the Accademia di Belle Arti in Venice and received the diploma in Fine Art

1942-46   taught at the Pacinotti Institute in Mestre

1946   set up own workshop as a sculptor

1957   won gold medal at the 2nd Triennial Exhibition, Milan

1960   opened the 'Salomon' garden at Solighetto for which he made giant iron sculptures

1965   won 1st prize Lindau international exhibition

1967   founded the Accademia Internazionale del Ferro at Marocco di Mogliano, Veneto

1977   won gold medal at Pontano-Naples exhibition

Exhibitions

1965, 1969, 1974 Lindau

1968   *Biennale d'arte sacra* Bologna, Rome, Milan

1968   *Scultura in ferro nella città domani* (one man show) Trieste

1970   *Sculpture of Toni Benetton* Milan Museum

Public Collections

Bad Godesberg: Protestant church
Belluno: Palazzo del Comune
Treviso: ironwork for Braida family tomb, the Palazzo dell' Administrazione Provinciale fountain in the Piazza S. Andrea sculpture in the Cathedral
Venice: Palazzo Grassi
Vicenza: gates for the cemetery

Simon Benetton

Publications

Gio Ponti *Domus* 1951, no 332
H. Scheel *Schmiede-und Schlosserarbeiten*
(Stuttgart 1959)
E. Roth *Neue Schmiede-und*
Schlosserarbeiten (Munich 1962)
P. Lopez *La Ferronnerie Italienne* (Milan
1969)

Exhibits

10* 'Transformazione' *(Transformation)*
1980
Cor Ten steel plate, gas cut. 1.40cm high x
1.05cm wide x 35cm thick. Colln. A.
Benetton

11 'La Sfera' *(Sphere)* 1966
Mild steel, gas cut. Approx diameter 4m.
The photograph shows Benetton's garden,
in which many of his matro-sculptures
are displayed. Colln. A. Benetton

208

Via Pagani Cesa 8, 31100 Treviso. Italy

1933   born in Treviso, Italy
Started working in his father
Antonio Benetton's workshop at an
early age, later attended the
Accademia di Belle Arti in Venice.
Taught sculpture at the Accademia
di Belle Arti in Macerata.
Runs own workshop in Treviso

Exhibitions

1958   *Maestri e giovani artisti Italiani*
Florence
1969   *International exhibition of Iron*
sculpture Imola
1976   *Design 76* Düsseldorf
1976   *International Exhibition* Musée
de Picardie, Amiens, France
1980   Lindau

Public Collections

Altura: sculpture for town centre
Trieste: Istituto Tecnico Industriale
Vicenza: Palazzo di Giustizia, Istitutto Tecnico
Geometre, Cassa di Risparmio, Ospedale Civile
Museums of Modern Art in Orleans, Turin,
Venice

Publications

Scultura Italiana Contemporanea Gabriele
Mandel (Milan 1965).
Il Mercato artistico Italiano 1800-1900
(Turin 1971).
Contemporary Iron and Metalwork Dona
Meilach (California 1976).
Simon Salvatore Maugeri (1981)

Exhibits

12* 'Ipotesi' (maquette for a sculpture)
1980
Cor Ten steel plate, oxyacetylene gas cut.
78cm high x 45cm wide x 30cm deep.
Colln. S. Benetton

13* 'Implicazione' (maquette for a
sculpture) 1980
Cor Ten steel plate, oxyacetylene gas cut.
85cm high x 35cm wide x 20cm deep.
Colln. S. Benetton

14* 'Estensione' (maquette for a sculpture)
1980
Cor Ten steel plate, oxyacetylene gas cut.
43cm high x 30cm wide x 30cm deep.
Colln. S. Benetton

Manfred Bergmeister

August-Birkmaier-Weg 2, 8019 Ebersberg bei München, W. Germany

1927	born in Ebersberg, Germany
1946-51	studied at the Meisterschule für Kunstschmiede in Munich and qualified as a journeyman blacksmith
1954	founded his workshop in Ebersberg, whose work included gates, railings, architectural fittings, and ecclesiastical items, particularly grave-crosses. His brother German (b.1937) works closely with him, having studied architectural metalwork and blacksmithing. The workshop now employs about 20 craftsmen
1955	qualified as a master blacksmith
1960	awarded the gold medal of the international handicrafts Fair in Munich
1981	awarded the Bavarian State Gold Medal for services to the community

Exhibitions

1956, 1960, 1965, 1969, 1974, 1980 Lindau International exhibition

Public Collections

Costermano war cemetery, Italy; Marigny war cemetery, France; Munich: Arabella park, St Helen's church, St Matthias war memorial cemetery, Town Hall; Nürnberg-Feucht; motorway restaurant

Publications

Stahl und Form Kunstschmiedearbeiten Manfred Bergmeister (1975 Munich)
Bronz und Stahl Manfred Bergmeister (1970 Bad Worishafen)

Exhibits

15* Lattice gates (photograph and section) 1981
Mild steel, the central member forged from one piece. The original design made for Munich Town Hall in 1977. 51cm high x 48.5cm wide x 4cm deep. Colln. M. Bergmeister

16 Grave-cross 1981
Forged bronze, partly chemically patinated, and partly gilded. 1.65cm high x 68cm wide x 20cm deep. Colln. M. Bergmeister

Manfred Bredohl

100 Aachen-Brand 20, W. Germany
Schmiedestr. 9

1944	born in Bergish-Gladbach, W. Germany
1964	journeyman's qualification
1967	graduated after 10 terms at the Fachhochschule, Aachen under Professor Fritz Ulrich, as a qualified designer
1969	opened own workshop in Aachen
1971	became a member of ADK (Arbeitsgemeinschaft des deutschen Kunsthandwerks)

Terrence Clark

1977 · gave two lecture tours in USA
1979-80 · travelled to Togo, Africa where he filmed smiths working.

Awards include many prizes in state competitions (1968-70-72-76-77)

Exhibitions

1973 · Aachen, Duisberg
1974 · *Geschmiedeter Stahl*
1976 · Düsseldorf
1980 · Lindau

Publications

Articles in *The Anvil's Ring* (Sept 1979, 1980, 1981) and *Lexikon der Zeitgenossischen Europäischen Künstler* (1980)

Exhibits

17* 'Schraubengitter' (*propellor gate*) 1970
Mild steel painted. 1.6m high x 63cm wide x 10cm deep. Colln. M. Bredohl

18* Window grille 1979
Mild steel. 76cm high x 76cm wide x 1cm deep. Colln. M. Bredohl

19* Candlestick 1980
Mild steel, painted. 42cm high x 13cm deep. Colln. M. Bredohl

20* 'Knoten' (section from a free standing grille)
Mild steel. 50cm high x approx 30cm diam. Colln. M. Bredohl

21* 'Kreis in Quadrat' (section of a room-divider) 1973
Mild steel. 1m high x 30cm wide x 13cm deep. Colln. M. Bredohl

22* 'Kussbaum' (section of a sculpture) 1979
Mild steel. 32cm high x 52cm wide x 24cm deep. Colln. M. Bredohl

David Courts   Pierre Degen

Wildfields Farm, Pound Lane,
Wood Street Village, nr Guildford, Surrey,
England

1946 born at Walton-on-Thames, Surrey
Apprenticed to a bookbinder; later
worked for an engineering firm
learning welding and fabrication
skills
1971 set up own business welding and
fabricating in steel for the
commercial market
1974 became involved in smithing.
1980 attended short design course at
Camberwell School of Art

Exhibits

23* Window Grille 1981
Mild steel, forged from solid section, the
interlocking joints welded. 1.5m high x 1m
wide x 10cm deep. Colln. T. Clark

24* Staircase balustrade (section)
Mild steel. 83cm high x 72cm wide x 10cm
deep. Colln. T. Clark

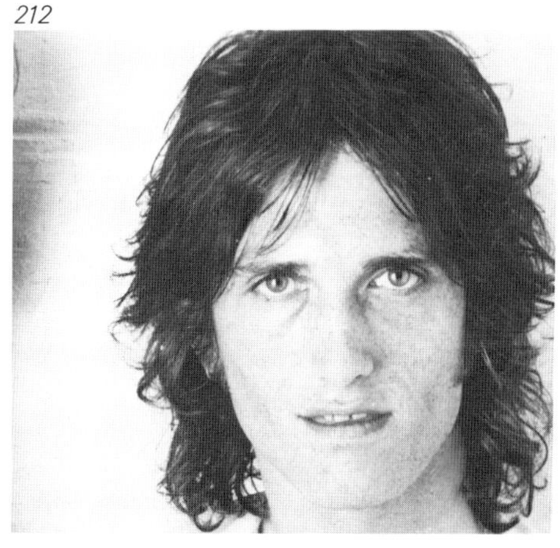

212

92 Heath Street, London NW3, England

1945 born in London
Studied at Hornsey College of Art
and Royal College of Art
1971 Joint Goldsmiths' Award.
Now works with W. Hackett

Exhibitions
1977 *Explosion; talent today* Goldsmiths'
Hall, London

Public Collections
V&A

Publications
Art in the 70s Edward Lucie-Smith (Oxford
1980)

Exhibit

25 Pin 1982 (drawing illustrated).
Steel, set with rubies; the unfolding plates of
enamelled 18ct gold. 9.2cm approx long x
2.1cm wide. Colln. D. Courts and W. Hackett

213

49 Grove Dwellings, Adelina Grove, London
E1, England

1947	born in La Neuveville, Switzerland
1963-68	studied at Ecole d'Arts Appliqués, Switzerland
1968-71	designed jewellery at 'Bucherer A G', La Chaux-de-Fonds Switzerland, and studied at the Kunstgewerbe Schule, Lucerne
1972, 1974 & 1976	scholarships from Bourse Fédérale des Arts Appliqués.Berne
1973	Diamond International Award
1977-78	taught at Bezald Academy of Art, Jerusalem
1979-81	taught at the Royal College of Art, London
1980-81	taught at Leicester, Ulster and Brighton Polytechnics, also Genit Rietveld Academie, Amsterdam
1973 to present	teacher and researcher in jewellery department of Middlesex Polytechnic,London

Charlotte De Syllas   John Dittmeier

Charlotte De Syllas

Exhibitions

1973	*The Craftsman's Art* V&A and Crafts Council, London
1973	*British Jewellers* Oslo and Bergen, Norway
1975, 1976	*Loot* Goldsmiths Hall, London
1977	*Craft in Question: New directions of the 70s* Whitworth Art Gallery, Manchester
1982	*The Maker's Eye* Craft Council, London

Public Collections

Royal Scottish Museum, Edinburgh and the Crafts Council, London

Publications

Contemporary Jewellery Ralph Turner (London 1976)
Creative Jewellery Patty Clarke (London 1978)
Goldschmiedekunst Reinhold Reiling (Koningsbach 1978)
Crafts Magazine 1979 no 38
1981 no 53

Exhibits

26* Hooking brooch 1977
Two steel rod triangles linked by blue, green and orange whipping thread. 3cm high x 8.5cm long. Colln. Crafts Council

27* Brooch 1978
Steel rod, orange nylon whipping thread and nickel tube in the form of a hanging triangle. 13.5cm long x 11.5cm wide. Colln. Crafts Council

28* Brooch 1977
Steel rod pyramid with orange nylon whipping thread, steel hook and green plastic tubing feet. 6.5cm long. Colln. Crafts Council

28 Park Avenue North, London N6, England

1946	born in Bridgetown, Barbados
1963-66	studied at Hornsey School of Art
1973-76	taught at the Royal College of Art

Exhibitions

1977	*Treasures of London* Vancouver and Montreal, Canada
1978	*Finger rings from Ancient Egypt to the present day* Oxford, Ashmolean Museum

Public Collections

Goldsmiths' Hall, London; Crafts Council

Exhibit

29* Necklace 1969
Blued steel, silver, and iolite; made of wire coiled, cut into links, interwoven and blued. The stones carved and held in place by bolting between settings. 11.5cm approx diam. Privately commissioned. Private Colln.

John Dittmeier

46 The Green, Dover, Delaware, DE 19901, USA

1951	born in Louisville, Kentucky, USA Has worked in forges in the USA and Britain

Publications

Various articles in the *Anvil's Ring*

Exhibits

30 Stand (section) 1981
Mild steel, forged, torch welded, filed and polished. 25.5 x 25.5 x 25.5cm. Colln. J. Dittmeier

31* Stand (photograph of drawing) 1981
Pencil. Height 45.5cm, Width 60cm. Colln. J. Dittmeier

Jan Dudesek

Ronald Eastman

215

34* Neckpiece 1981
Stainless steel, made out of one piece. 15cm approx diameter. Colln. J. Dudesek

35* Candlestick 1980
Mild steel. 25cm high. Colln. J. Dudesek

36* Grave-cross 1982
Cor-ten steel. 1.85m high x 50cm wide. Colln. J. Dudesek

216

Burgschmiede, 8124 Maur, Switzerland

1946	born in Pardubiče, Czechoslovakia Studied architecture in Prague
1969	Set up independent workshop in Switzerland
1980	awarded prize of the city of Lindau

Exhibitions

1978-81	Basle mixed exhibition
1980	Lindau

Exhibits

32* Griddle with stand 1980
Mild steel. 40cm high. Colln. J. Dudesek

33* Fire-irons with stand 1980
Mild steel. 65cm high. Colln. J. Dudesek

Richard Quinnell Ltd, Rowhurst Forge, Oxshott Road, Leatherhead, Surrey, England

1932	born in California USA Trained with Quinnell Ltd and on CoSIRA courses
Since 1961	foreman blacksmith with R Quinnell's

Public Collections
Liverpool, Anglican Cathedral (West gates and screen); Bowood House, Calne (arboretum gates)

Exhibit

37 Car-park barrier (section) 1982
Mild steel, painted. Approx 50cm high x 50cm wide x 40cm deep. Colln. Richard Quinnell Ltd

Alan Evans   Hermann Gradinger

Makins, Whiteway, Stroud, Gloucestershire,
England

1952	born in Gloucestershire
1970-73	Studied at Shoreditch College of Education
1974-78	worked with Alan Knight in Worcestershire, on both large scale pieces and jewellery
1978	set up own workshop in Gloucestershire
1981	won limited competition for entrance gates to new Crypt Treasury, St Paul's Cathedral, London

Exhibitions
1982   *The Maker's Eye* Crafts Council

Publications
Crafts Magazine January 1982

Exhibits

38* Firegrate 1981
Mild steel. 45.5cm wide x 29cm deep x
17.5cm high. Commissioned by the Crafts
Council for this exhibition. Colln. A. Evans

39* Pair of firedogs 1979
Mild steel, waxed. 43cm high x 66cm wide.
Colln. A. Evans

40* Doorknocker 1980
Mild steel, lacquered. 25.5cm high x 5.5cm
wide x 6.5cm deep. Colln. A. Evans

**41* Gates to St Paul's Cathedral
Treasury** (photograph) 1981
Mild steel plate and bar cut, forged, welded
and rivetted; the surface finished by shot-
blasting, wire brushing and lacquering. 2.7m
high x 3.6m wide. Commissioned by the
Dean and Chapter of St Paul's Cathedral, with
the help and encouragement of the Crafts
Council

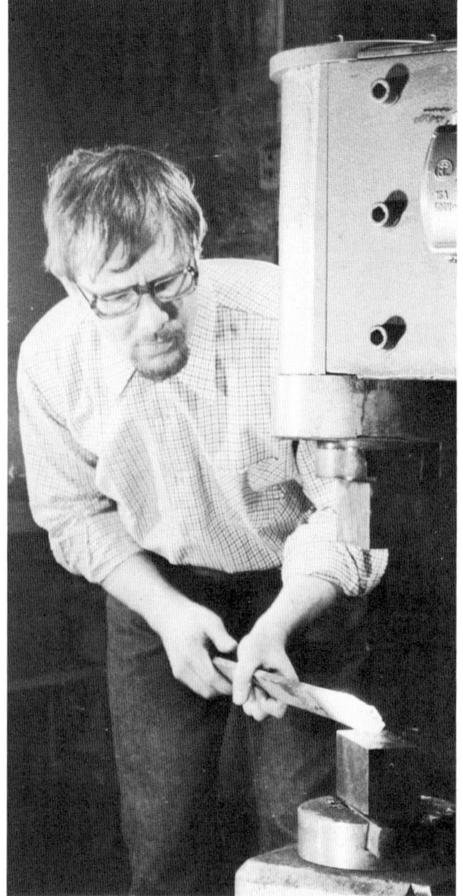

217

Grabenstrasse 53, 6500 Mainz —
Gensenholm, West Germany

1936	born in Mainz, Germany
1953-55	apprentice locksmith
1955	journeyman's certificate in locksmithing
1956-61	work in various workshops
1961	studied at the Meisterschule für Bau-und Kunstschlosser

Martha Gumn Alfred Habermann

(locksmithing) under Prof. Edwin Roth

1962	Master's certificate
1966	took over father's workshop
1972	State prize for fine craftwork in Rheinland-Pfalz

Exhibitions
1965, 69, 74, 80 Lindau
1974 *Welding in Art*, Aachen
1977 *Exemplat 77*: Crafts and the Church, Munich

Publications
Entwurfsmappen für Kunstschmiedearbeiten Coleman-Verlag, (Lübeck 1970)
Schmiede + Schlosserarbeiten von heute (Stuttgart 1974)
Dekorative Türen (Stuttgart 1976)
Gärten- & Einfahrtstore, Gittertüren (Stuttgart 1978)
Schmiedeeisen am Haus und in der Umwelt (Budapest, Hungary 1981)

Exhibits

42 Window grille 1982
Mild steel forged with a power hammer from a flat bar 40cm x 80cm and welded. 1.80m high x 1.20m wide. Colln. H. Gradinger

43* Door grille (section) 1982
Mild steel, forged from square bars 20 x 88mm. 1.20m high x 55cm wide. Colln. H. Gradinger

44* Staircase bannisters (photograph) 1980
Mild steel. Colln. Town Hall Mainz-Gonsenheim

Unit 268, 27 Clerkenwell Close, London EC1, England

1955 born in Over Wallop, Hampshire, England
Studied at Central School of Art and Design
Teaches at Southwark College and Morley College

Exhibitions
1980, 1981 *Loot* Goldsmiths' Hall
1981 *New Faces* British Craft Centre
1981 *Black Jewellery* Oxford Gallery

Public Collections
Goldsmiths' Hall, V&A.

Exhibits

45 Ring 1981
Mild steel and silver, matt polished and waxed. Diam 3.5mm. Colln. M. Gumn

46* Bangle 1981
Mild steel, silver and nickel, matt polished and waxed. Diam 10mm. Colln. V&A

47 Ring 1981
Mild steel and silver, matt polished and waxed. Diam 3.5cm. Colln. M. Gumn

---

378-56 Studena, c. 304 okr Jindr Hradec, Czechoslovakia

1930 born in Jihlava, Czechoslovakia
Son of a blacksmith, trained as an industrial blacksmith, then later started and directed a new state workshop for restoration work in Jihlava; now chief restorer for ironwork for historical monuments in Czechoslovakia; awarded the title Master Craftsman in Old Crafts

1975 founded his own workshop in a small village outside Studena. Invitations to work abroad have come from East and West Germany, Italy, Japan and Wales.

1981 artist/craftsman in residence at Dyfed College of Art, Wales

Exhibitions
1964, Berlin, Budapest, Cairo, Havana,
1980 Lindau, Munich, Prague.

Publications
Numerous, including *Der Schlosser*

Public Collections
Museum of Fine Arts, Brno, Czechoslovakia; Dyfed County Council Museum, Abergwili, Wales

Exhibit

48 Pair of gates 1975
Iron. 2.60m high x 2.50m wide x 0.20m diam. Colln. Town of Trest, Czechoslovakia

Illustration overleaf

218

219

18 Camden Road, London NW1, England

1949	born in England
	Studied at Hornsey College of Art and Royal College of Art
1974	British Steel Award
	Now works with D. Courts

Exhibitions

1977   *Explosion; talent today* Goldsmiths' Hall, London

Public Collections

V&A

Publications

Art in the 70s Edward Lucie-Smith (Oxford 1980)

Exhibit

25* Pin 1982 (drawing illustrated)
Steel, set with rubies; the unfolding plates of enamelled 18ct gold. 9.2cm approx long x 2.1cm approx wide. Colln. D. Courts and W. Hackett

Claydon Forge, Claydon, Suffolk, England

1943	born in Bromley, Kent, England
1973-75	worked with welding firm in Kent
1976	attended CoSIRA course
1977	set up own workshop at Claydon
1980	organisers' award at Lindau International Exhibition
1982	Workshipful Company of Blacksmiths' Diploma for work of outstanding merit

Exhibitions

1980	Lindau
1982	*The Maker's Eye* Crafts Council

Public Collections

V&A

Exhibits

49* Design for sunburst firescreen 1981
Ink on tracing paper. 70cm high x 46cm wide. Colln. S. Hill

50* Firebasket 1981
Mild steel, made from a single piece of steel plate cut, twisted and folded into shape. 30.5cm high x 76cm long x 33cm wide. Colln. S. Hill

51* Sunburst firescreen 1981
Mild steel, made from a single piece of steel plate cut, and fanned into shape. 63.5cm high x 91.5cm wide. Colln. S. Hill

52 Blue fence (section) 1980
Mild steel made from 25mm x 50mm tube, painted. Approx 122cm square. Colln. S. Hill

53* Millbank fence (section) 1981-2
Mild steel; angle iron, gas cut, twisted and
painted. approx 82.5cm high x 3m long x
12.5cm deep. Commissioned by the
architects Chapman, Taylor and Partners for
the new Metropolitan Police Administration
Headquarters, Millbank, London

Elizabeth Holder James Horrobin

7 Lavender Gdns, London SW11, England

1950	born in Sindelfingen, W. Germany
1977-78	Fachhochschule, Düsseldorf
1978-80	awarded *Preis der deutscher Kunsthandwerker* and apprenticed in jewellery in the workshops of Wener Thiele and Alfred Weichert
1978-80	Royal College of Art

Exhibitions

| 1981 | *Sideshow* ICA London |
| 1981 | Electrum Gallery, London |

Publications

Crafts Magazine October 1981

Public Collections

Schmuckmuseum, Pforzheim; Goldschmiedehaus, Hanau; North West Arts Association

Exhibits

54* Neckpiece 1981
Blued sprung steel with alabaster disc. 14cm wide x 12cm deep x 32mm high. Colln. E. Holder

55* Bracelet
Sprung steel, the cross-over clasp in 18ct gold. 6.8cm max diam. Colln. Crafts Council

56* Bracelet
Sprung steel, the triangular clasp of bronze. 6.8cm max diam. Colln. Crafts Council

---

Laurel Cottage Forge, Carhampton, Minehead, Somerset, England

1946	born in Stafford, England
1961-66	apprenticed to his father Harry Horrobin, blacksmith; attended metalwork courses at Hereford Technical College.
1969	set up own workshop in Watchet, Somerset
1981	part-time lecturer, West Surrey College of Art.
1981	won commission from V&A for pair of gates for museum's ironwork gallery.

Exhibitions

| 1979 | *Bowl Exhibition* British Crafts Centre, London |
| 1982 | *'The Maker's Eye'* Crafts Council |

Public Collections

V&A; Kirkham House (Dept of Environment Ancient Monument)

Exhibits

57* Fire-basket 1980
Mild steel. 30cm high x 110cm long x 33cm wide. Colln. V&A

58* Garden gate 1980
Mild steel. 180cm high x 100cm wide x 10cm deep. Commissioned by Rachel Reckitt of Minehead, Somerset. Colln. R. Reckitt

59* Gates for V&A Ironwork Gallery (photograph) 1981-2
Mild steel. Commissioned as the result of a limited competition held by the V&A in conjunction with the DoE. Colln. V&A

---

60 Maquette of proposed design for gates to St Paul's Cathedral Treasury 1981
Mild steel. 60cm high x 100cm wide x 30cm deep. Designed for limited competition held by Dean and Chapter of St Paul's Cathedral. Colln. J. Horrobin

61 Sample detail (full size) of proposed St Paul's gates 1981
Mild steel. 60cm high x 45cm wide x 30cm deep. Colln. J. Horrobin

62* Bowl 1979
Mild steel. Diam 25cm. Private Colln.

63 Fire-grate 1981
Mild steel. 35cm high x 73cm long x 42.5cm wide. Commissioned by the Crafts Council for this exhibition

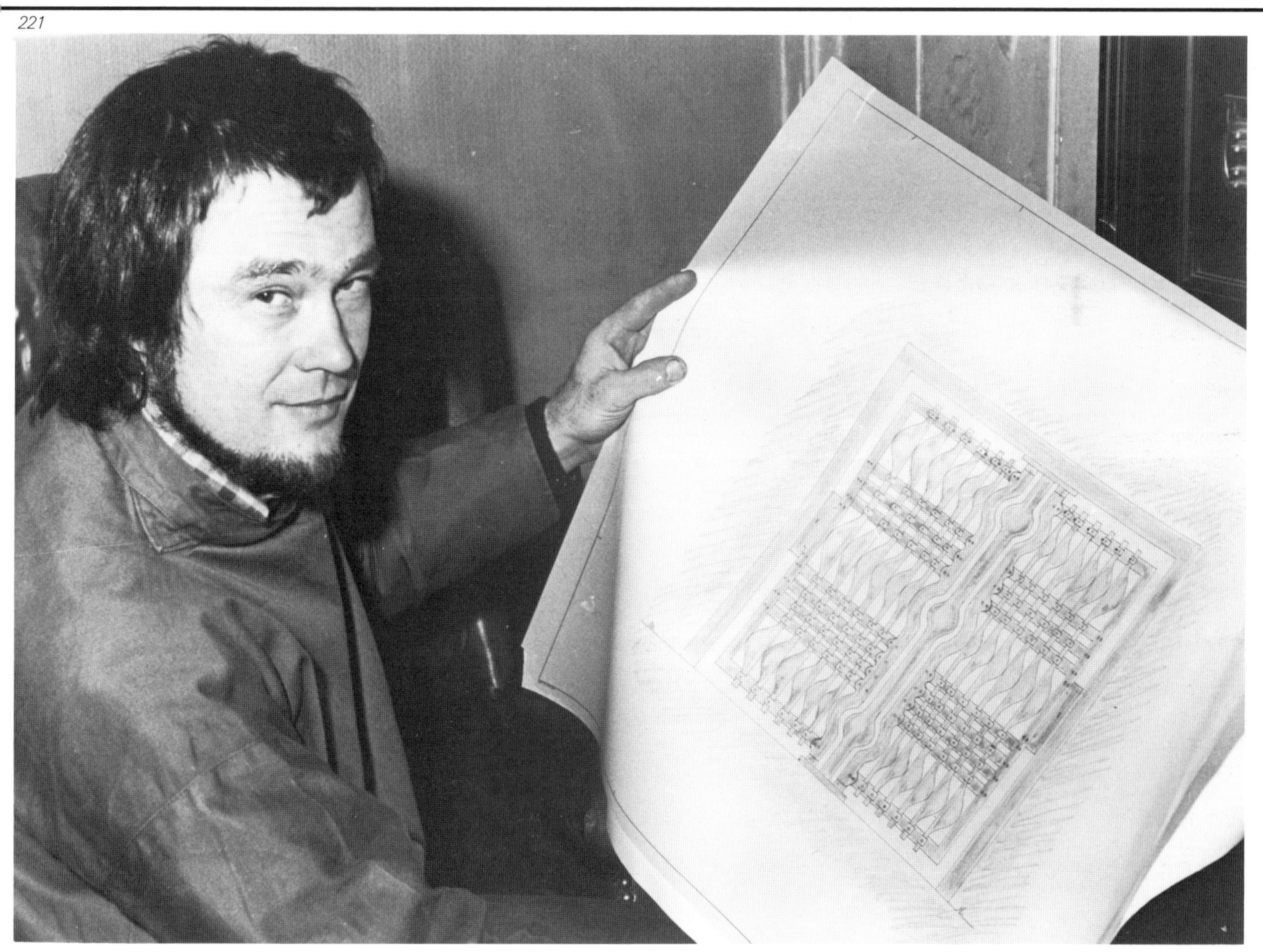

Walfrid Huber

Robert Hutchinson

222

A – 2222 Pirawarth 396, Austria

1942	born in Austria
1975	Academy of Fine Arts, Vienna diploma in sculpture

Seven years' experience as a locksmith's and blacksmith's journeyman.

Exhibitions

1977	*House of Artists* Kunstlerhaus, Vienna
1978	*Z* Centralbank, Vienna

Public Collections

Province of Lower Austria

Publications

Sculpture live, Vienna, Kunstlerhaus, 1980

Exhibit

64* 'Die Maschinenwesen' 1978
(photograph)
Mild steel, forged and welded. 1.5m high x 80cm long. Colln. Westentaschenmuseum, Austria

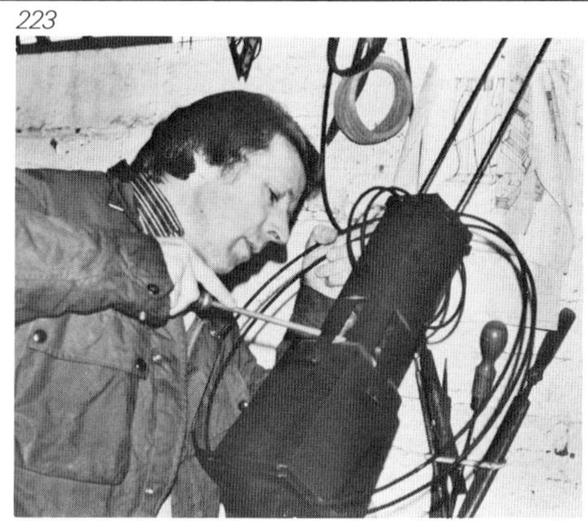

223

Kippen Forge, Kippen, Stirlingshire, Scotland

1936	born in London, England Studied at Edinburgh College of Art and Leith Technical College – courses in silversmithing and lettering
1952-55	apprenticeship in the drawing office and practical metalworking at Edinburgh architectural metalworkers Charles Henshaw & Sons Ltd
1960-68	designer/estimator with Glasgow firm of architectural metalworkers Kingeton Brass Co., Ltd.
1968	set up own workshop

Exhibition

1975	One man shows in Edinburgh and Glasgow

Exhibit

65* Gate 1980
Mild steel forged and assembled, using an electric welder, and painted black. 91.5cm high x 91.5cm wide x 5cm deep. Made for Tom Inglis. Colln. Tom Inglis

Louis Brent Kington

224

Rural Route 1, Box 91 D, Makanda, Illinois 62958, USA

1934	born in Kansas, USA
1957	BA in Fine Art University of Kansas
1961	MA in Fine Art Cranbrook Academy of Art
1961-72	taught at School of Art, Southern Illinois University
Since 1972	Professor in the School of Art, Southern Illinois University, Carbondale, Ill

Exhibitions

1971	*Design in Steel Awards; American Iron and Steel Institute* New York, NY
1976	*Wind and Weathervanes* Los Angeles Craft and Folk Museum, Ca
1978	*American Crafts for the Vatican Museum* the Vatican City, Rome

Public Collections

Minnesota Museum of Art, St. Paul, MN
Evansville Museum of Art, Evansville, IN
Museum of American Crafts, New York, NY
Museum and Art Galleries, Southern Illinois University, Carbondale, IL

Exhibits

66* Weathervane 'Icarus 5' 1981
Mild steel, forged oxyacetylene gas-welded and polychromed. 85.1cm high x 63.5cm wide x 81.3cm (diam). Colln. L. Brent Kington

67* Weathervane 1981
Mild steel, oxyacetelene gas-welded, and painted. 109.3cm high x 63.5cm wide x 81.3cm (diam). Colln. L. Brent Kington

Takayoshi Komine

225

Atelier Yukazan, 366 Kitaiwaoka, Tokorozawa-shi, Saitama-ken, Japan

1950	born in Tokyo MA (Metalwork), Musashino Art University, Tokyo.
1977-79	Practical experience in West Germany; the smiths with whom he worked there include Bergmeister and Zimmermann

Exhibition

1980	Lindau

Exhibits

68* Bookrests A 1981
Forged and waxed steel, each made from one piece. 23cm high x 13cm wide x 23cm diam. Colln. Takayoshi Komine

69* Bookrests B 1981
Forged and waxed steel, each rest made from one piece. 18cm high x 20cm wide x 18cm diam. Colln. Takayoshi Komine

70* Bookrests D 1981
Forged and waxed steel, made from one piece. 23cm high x 15cm wide x 15cm diam. Colln. Takayoshi Komine

Achim Kühn

Atelier für Stahl-und Metallgestaltung,
1185 Berlin-Altglienicke, Richterstrasse 6,
East Germany

1942	born in Berlin, Germany
1956-59	apprenticed in father's workshop, taking over the workshop in 1967, after the latter's sudden death
1963-72	part-time training as an architect
1971	member of the VBK of the DDR

Exhibitions

1969	Berlin
1972	Erfurt
1971, 1979	Lindau
1977	Karl-Marx-Stadt
1979	Moscow
1980	Theatre of 'Palast der Republik', and an exhibition of lights by Fritz and Achim Kühn in Schmokwitz (Berlin)

Exhibits

71 'Schwingender Stahl' (*Swinging steel*)
(section and photograph of complete screen)
1976
Steel forged with hardened high-grade steel,
complete piece composed of 12 single
pieces and a base plate. 2.3m high x 5m
wide x 300mm deep (complete object).
Colln. Achim Kühn

72* 'Verdrehung' (*Torsion*) 1977
Forged steel. 150m high x 1.7m diameter
(excluding base). Colln. Zentralforschungs-
intitut Rossendorf/GDR

73* Sculpture 1975
Forged steel, high-grade steel welded and
sledge hammered. 2.3m high x 400mm
wide x 400mm diam. Colln. Museum fur
Kunsthandwerk (Grassi-Museum), Leipzig

Fritz Kühn

227

1910	born in Berlin, died 1967
1924-28	studied tool-making, lock-smithing and blacksmithing in his father's workshop, whilst attending evening classes at the Berlin School of Craftsmen
1937	became a master locksmith, establishing a forge in Grünau
1941	he held his first one-man show in Berlin
1943-49	workshop was destroyed in the war and then reconstructed
1954	awarded the National Prize for Arts and Literature of the German Democratic Republic
1958	took part in the German pavilion at the World Fair in Brussels
1964	the East German Ministry of Culture nominated him a professor. Kühn's reputation was considerable for his work as a photographer, as well as a blacksmith

Publications

Geschmiedetes Eisen F Kühn (Berlin 1939)
Geschmiedetes Gerat F Kühn (Berlin 1954)
Eisen und Stahl F Kühn (Berlin 1957)
Stahl und Metallarbeiten F Kühn (Berlin 1959)
Wrought iron F Kühn (London 1965)
Decorative Work in wrought iron and other metals F Kühn (London 1967)

Exhibitions

1941	Numerous one-man shows of both ironwork and photography
1956	One-man exhibition (Berlin, Markisches Museum)
	Fritz Kühn the blacksmith as photographer Potsdam
1964	Essen, Folkwang Museum

Ian Lamb

1969   *Fritz Kühn* Paris Musée des arts decoratifs

1970   *Memorial exhibition: Ideasta Teoksen* Helsinki Arts Hall

Public Collections
Lindau

Exhibits

74* Panels from Entrance doors to Berlin City Library (section and photograph of complete doors, which show 117 different types of the letter 'A'.) 1965.
Forged steel, enamelled copper, gold leaf. 1.4m high x 1.25m wide x 40cm diameter. Colln. Achim Kühn

75* Bowl: 'Erstarrte Bewegung' (*frozen movement*)
Forged steel. 40cm diameter. Colln. Achim Kühn

76* 'Drei Bunde' (*three bands*) 1964
Mild steel, forged. 1.67m high x 60cm wide. Colln. Achim Kühn

77* Bowl: 'Zinnie' (*zinnia*)
Forged and pickled steel. 40cm diameter. Colln. Achim Kühn

228

Richard Quinnell Ltd, Rowhurst Forge, Oxshott Road, Leatherhead, Surrey, England

1934   born in Montrose, Scotland Apprenticeship with Richard Quinnell Ltd; attended CoSIRA courses

Public Collections
Greenwich Royal Observatory (Corona)
Bristol & West Building Society, Broadquay, Bristol (Weathervane)

Exhibit

78* Group of three forged grilles 1981
Mild steel, burnished and waxed.
82cm high x 61cm wide x 30cm deep.
Colln. Fire & Iron Gallery

Robert Legg

93 Gayton House, Knapp Road, London E3, England

1946   born in Birmingham; England
1960-66   Apprenticed as hand-engraver/die-sinker to W W Allen, in the print industry; worked as die-sinker, and later with a firm of engravers and photo-etchers
1973-76   studied silversmithing and jewellery at City of Birmingham Polytechnic and the Royal College of Art
1980   researched surface decoration on gold and silver, using machine technology, at the Sir John Cass School of Art

Public Collection
Crafts Council

Exhibit

79 Hand mirror 1978
Mild steel, blued; turned with carved and engraved interwoven fish forms inlaid with fine gold. Diam 7.4cm. Colln. Crafts Council

Maurice Long Jan Brooks Loyd

20 Grafton Crescent, London, NW1, England

1959	born in London Studied silversmithing and metalwork at Camberwell School of Art and Crafts
1981	2nd prize, Johnson Matthey Metals Silver Award

Publications

In *Crafts Magazine* November 1981

Exhibit

80* Firebasket 1981

Mild steel. 73.5cm high x 48cm long x 39cm wide. Commissioned by the Crafts Council for this exhibition. Colln. M. Long

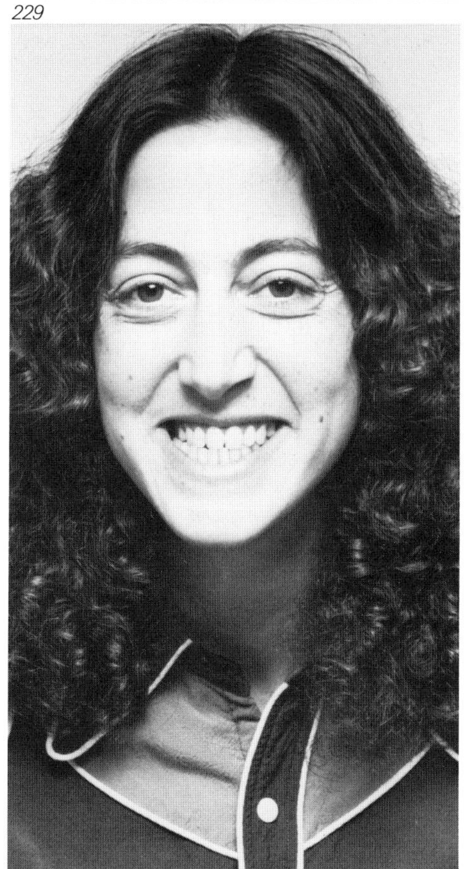

229

PO Box 264, Newell, North Carolina 28126, USA

1950	born in Quanah, Texas
1972	BA Southern Illinois University, Carbondale
1974	MFA Southern Illinois University, Carbondale
1974-77	taught Southern Illinois University
1977-78	taught University of North
1982	Carolina, Charlotte, North Carolina
1979	Carolina Designer-Craftsmen award, N.C. Museum of Art, Raleigh, North Carolina

Exhibitions

1974	*Goldsmith '74* Renwick Gallery, Smithsonian, Washington & tour
1974	*Forms in metal; 275 years of metalsmithing in America* (touring)
1976	*Designer-craftsmen 1976* Richmond Art Centre, Richmond, Calif
1979-80	*Contemporary Crafts* Southern Arts touring programme
1979	*Blacksmithing USA* Craftsmen's Gallery Omaha, Nebraska Norfolk Art Centre, Norfolk, Nebraska
1981	*Blacksmithing '81* Gallery of Contemporary Metalsmithing Rochester, NY

Publications

Contemporary Crafts of the Americas Nila Getty 1975
Tradition and Change; the new American Craftsman Julie Hall 1978

Public Collections

Arkansas Arts Centre, Southern Illinois University Museum, Carbondale University of Georgia, National Ornamental Metal Museum, Memphis

Exhibit

81* 'Crossed Signals' 1981

Mild steel, variously coloured. 33cm max diam. Colln. J. Brooks Loyd

Giuseppe Lund

4 Lower Road, Harmer Hill, Shrewsbury,
Salop, England

1951	born in United Kingdom studied Philosophy at Bristol and Southampton Universities and music at the Royal College of Music
1974	trained with Anthony Robinson and attended a CoSIRA course
1976	set up own workshop in Brockenhurst, Hants
1977	toured Continent visiting blacksmiths in France, Germany, Italy
1979-80	in partnership with A. Robinson

Exhibitions
1980   Lindau

Publications
In *Crafts Magazine* August 1979

Exhibits

82* Firebasket 1981
Iron and mild steel. 73.5cm high x 48cm long x 39cm wide. Commissioned by the Crafts Council for the exhibition. Colln. G. Lund

83* Spiral Staircase (section) 1982
Mild steel. Approx 167cm high x 167cm wide. Colln. G. Lund

84* Gates 1981
Mild steel, the surface untreated. Approx 183cm high x 122cm wide. Colln. G. Lund

85 Grillework (section) 1981
Mild steel. Approx 185cm high x 93cm wide. Colln. G. Lund

230

Serge Marchal Hiroshi Minamizawa Denys Mitchell

231

34 bis rue Mareschal, 3000 Nimes, France

1944	born near Paris, France
1961-64	studied at the Ecole des Arts Decoratifs de Grenoble
1964-66	apprenticed as locksmith-cum-blacksmith to Daniel Souriou at Nimes
1968-71	continued training with the Compagnons du Devoir, working in different training centres throughout France
1971	qualified as a master locksmith with the Compagnons du Devoir
1977	set up own workshop

Exhibitions
1980   Lindau

Exhibits

86 Vent 1980
Mild steel, varnished. 50cm high x 1.3m wide x 22cm deep. Colln. S. Marchal

232

Nishijo, Kameoka-shi, Kyoto-fu, Japan

| 1933 | born in Kyoto, Japan Educated in Kyoto Three times prizewinner at the Kyoto Craft Exhibition |

Exhibitions
| 1969, 1971 | Hanshin Dept. Store Gallery, Osaka |
| 1960-73 | Kyoto Craft Exhibitions: thereafter judging this exhibition |

Publications
Tetsunokogei (Iron Craft) 1976

Exhibits

87* Screen: 'Waves at Sea': (section showing 2 panels from 6-panel original) 1982
Mild steel. 270cm high x 230cm wide x 6cm diam. Colln. Hiroshi Minamizawa

88* Screen: 'Stream' 1981
Mild steel. 175cm high x 170cm wide x 3cm diam. Colln. Hiroshi Minamizawa

233

Ragged School Forge, Kelso, Scotland

1939	born in Hatton, Aberdeenshire Trained on CoSIRA courses under tutorship of Ivan Smith
1974	set up workshop as part-time smith
1976	became full-time smith

Exhibitions
Scottish Crafts Come to America Virginia USA

Art and Craft in Scotland Luxembourg

Exhibit

89* Railing (full-size sample) 1981
Mild steel, finished in matt black. The head ornaments flame cut, the uprights attached by welding. Approx 214cm high x 183cm long x 61cm deep. The original screen and double gates were commissioned by the Standard Life Assurance Company for the courtyard of their head office in George Street, Edinburgh. Colln. D. Mitchell

Kauko Moisio

Martin Page

Vanha Meilahti 2, 00270 Helsinki 27, Finland

1928	born at Ypaja, Finland Trained in Helsinki at Taideteollinen Oppilaitos; Taidetakojan ja metallopakot- tajien koulu
1966-67	Werkkunstschule der Stadt, Aachen
1969 1981	State artist award

Exhibitions

1967	Goethe Institut Helsinki
1969	Gallerie Artek Helsinki
1973	Aamos Andersson Museum Helsinki
1976-77	Kunstambaght vormgeving, Belgium
1980	Lindau

Public Collections
City of Helsinki, Finland

Publications
Avotakka 1977

Exhibit

90* Dining Chair 1981
Stainless steel and leather. 68cm high x
52.5cm wide x 46cm diam. Colln. K. Moisio

4 Vicars Road, London NW5, England

1952	born in Pembroke Dock, South Wales
1968-70	Shrewsbury School of Art
1970-73	Central School of Art and Design
1973-76	Royal College of Art
1976	British Steel Melchett Award Teaches at Epsom School of Art

Exhibitions

1977	V&A *Presentation Pieces*
1979	*One-man show* Electrum Gallery London
1979, 1980	*Loot* Goldsmiths' Hall

Public Collections
V&A; Goldsmiths' College

Exhibits

91* Pair of earrings
Mild steel, etched, with gold dots. Diam 3cm
x 4.5cm long. Colln. M. Page

92* Pair of earrings
Mild steel and gold leaf. Diam 1.7cm x
7.9cm long. Colln. M. Page

235

Albert Paley

236

335 Aberdeen Street, Rochester, New York 14619, USA

1944	born in Philadelphia, USA
1962-66	BA in Fine Art from the Tyler School of Art, Temple University, Philadelphia, Penn.
1966-69	MA in Fine Art from the Tyler School of Art, Temple University, Philadelphia, Penn.
1968-69	taught at Tyler School of Art
1969-72	taught at the School for American Craftsmen, Rochester Institute of Technology, Rochester, New York
since 1972	teaches at New York State University College at Brockport, New York
1975	Design in Steel Award, American Iron and Steel Institute of America
1975	Lilian Fairchild Award, University of Rochester, New York
1976	National Endowment of the Arts master apprenticeship grant
1976	National Endowment of the Arts craftsman fellowship grant

Paley began work as a jeweller, later moving to large-scale work in steel and bronze. He has recently been commissioned to design lamp-posts, tree-gratings and benches for Pennsylvania Avenue in Washington DC

Exhibitions

1970-73	*International Jewellery Exhibition* Munich
1970	*Goldsmiths 70* New York Museum of Contemporary Crafts
1974	*Goldsmiths '74* Washington, DC Renwick Gallery, Smithsonian Institution
1975	*Forms in metal* New York Museum of Contemporary Crafts
1975	*Goldsmithing exhibition* Mexico City, Universidad Nacional Autonoma de Mexico
1976	*International Jewellery Art* Tokyo Nihon Keizal Shimbun
1976	*The Blacksmith as an artist and craftsman in the US* Carbondale, Southern Illinois University
1977	*Solid Wrought USA* New York Museum of Contemporary Crafts
1978	*Craft, Art and Religion* Smithsonian Institution, Washington DC and the Vatican Museum, Rome
1979	*Paley/Castle/Wildenhain* Memorial Art Gallery, Rochester, New York
1980	*The Metalwork of Albert Paley* John Michael Kohler Arts Center, Sheboygan, Wisconsin and Hunter Museum of Art, Chattanooga
1981	*Albert Paley – the paradox of iron* Fendwick Gallery, Washington DC

Public Collections

Temple University, Philadelphia;
Memorial Art Gallery, University of Rochester, New York;
Minnesota Museum of Art, St Paul, Minnesota;
Renwick Gallery, Smithsonian Institution, Washington DC;
Hunter Art Museum, Chattanooga, Tennessee;
Helen Drutt Gallery, Philadelphia, Penn.

Peter Parkinson

Publications

The Art of Jewellery (London 1972) Graham Hughes

Body Jewellery Donald Willcox (New York 1973)

Metal Techniques for Craftsmen Oppi Untracht (London 1974)

Contemporary Jewellery: a critical reassessment Ralph Turner 1945-75 (London 1976)

Ornamental and Defensive Ironwork Michael Southworth (Boston 1977)

Decorative and Sculptural Ironwork Dona Meilach (New York 1977)

Exhibits

93* Railing 1981
Mild steel, with rusted surface. 2.7m long x 2.4m high x 20cm deep. Colln. A. Paley

94* Pair of andirons 1981
Mild steel. 60cm high x 60cm wide approx. Colln. A. Paley

95* Two plant-stands 1981
Mild steel. Each approx 50cm diameter, 1.5m high. Colln. A. Paley

96* Chattanooga Fence (photograph) 1975
Mild steel. Approx 26m long x 1.8-3.45m high. Colln. Hunter Museum of Art, Chattanooga, Tennessee

97 Rectilinear gate 1982
Mild steel. Approx 2.1m long x 1.5 high. Colln. A. Paley

237

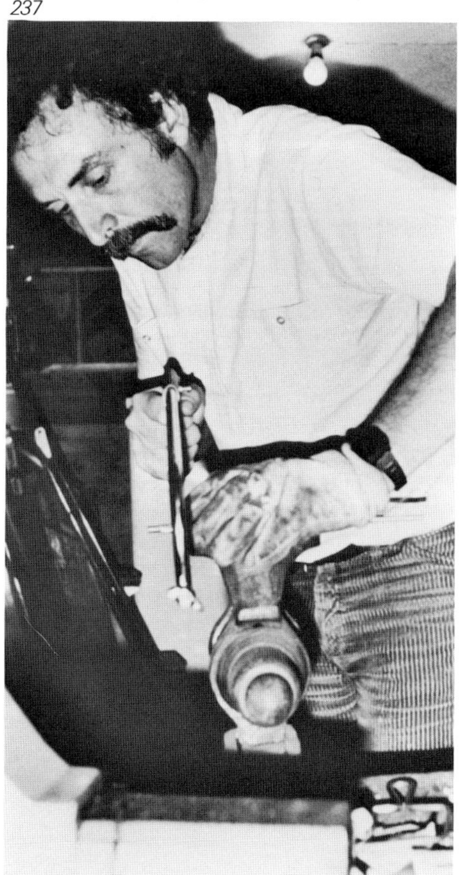

Bronte Cottage, Barley Mow Hill, Arford, Headley Bardon, Hampshire, England

1942	born in Oswestry, Salop, England
1960-64	studied at Royal College of Art
1964-66	industrial designer, London Transport Architects Dept.
1966-68	industrial designer, Allied Ironfounders
1968-69	part-time lecturer, Guildford School of Art
1969-82	lecturer, West Surrey College of Art and Design
1980	blacksmithing experience in workshop of Richard Quinnell

Exhibitions

1981	Cranleigh Arts Centre

Exhibits

98* Firegrate 1981
Mild steel and brass, finished with graphite and silicone wax. 16cm high x 55.5cm wide x 46cm deep. One of a group specially commissioned for this exhibition by the Crafts Council

99 Bowl no 1 1980
Mild steel, blocked and raised from 3/16in plate at red heat. Diam 17.8cm x 5.1cm deep. Colln. P. Parkinson

100* Candleholder 1980
Mild steel, forged and rivetted. 35.5cm high. Colln. P. Parkinson

101 Bowl no 2 1980
Mild steel, forged, welded and the surface heat treated to form *fire texture* which is enhanced by using phosphoric acid pickle. Diam 22.9cm x 11.5cm deep. Colln. P. Parkinson

102* Bowl no 3 1980
Mild steel, formed as no 101. Diam 22.3cm x 9cm deep. Colln. P. Parkinson

103* Bowl no 4 1980
Mild steel, blocked and raised from ¼in plate at red heat. The pattern etched into the bowl with nitric acid. Diam 25.4cm. Colln. P. Parkinson

Middle Farm House, Rotten Row,
Theddlethorpe, Mabelthorpe, Lincolnshire,
England

1948	born in Moscow
1966-67	Bournemouth College of Art
1970	graduated in jewellery design from Hornsey College of Art
1973-74	set up own jewellery workshop with the help of a Crafts Council grant
1976	moved to present workshop, and spent time working in nearby forge of John Joyce and Fred Phillipson
1978	six-month craft residency in Australia
1981	research fellowship at Sheffield City Polytechnic

Exhibitions

1975   *Jewellery in Europe* Scottish Arts Council/Crafts Council (touring exhibition)

1982   *The Maker's Eye* Crafts Council, London

Public Collections
V&A; Crafts Council

Publications
Contemporary Jewellery: a critical assessment Ralph Turner
World of the Makers Edward Lucie-Smith

Exhibits

104 Necklace 1980
Stainless steel, forged, filed and polished by hand; tapered with a slight angle at the front. Max diam 14.2cm. Colln. D. Poston

105* Necklace 1980
Stainless steel, forged, filed and polished by hand, with acutely angled front. Max diam 14.3cm. Colln. D. Poston

106* Necklace with hook 1981
Stainless steel, forged, filed and polished; made from one piece. Max diam 13.5cm. Colln. D. Poston

107* Firebowl
Mild steel; made from two sheets of ½in steel plate, formed with a ten-pound sledge hammer. 27cm high x 52cm long x 40cm wide. Commissioned by the Crafts Council for this exhibition. Designed by David Poston, made by him with Ian Lamb and Eammon Kenward (of Richard Quinnell Ltd). Colln. D. Poston and R. Quinnell

108* Necklace 1980
Stainless steel, forged, filed and polished by hand. Made from one piece. Colln. V&A Museum no M49-1980

109* Bracelet 1981
Stainless steel, forged, filed and polished by hand. Max diam 8.4cm. Colln. D. Poston

239

Anthony Robinson

Rowhurst Forge, Oxshott Road, Leatherhead,
Surrey, England

1940	born in Leatherhead
1963	BA in Natural Sciences, Cambridge University
1975	managing director of Richard Quinnell Ltd
1978	Winston Churchill Memorial Fellowship

Exhibits

110* 'Isolink' 1982
Mild steel, hot formed and fabricated, flame
metallized with zinc and painted. 1.50m high
x 2m long x 1.20m deep. Made as a result of
the practical help and encouragement of the
director of BKL Fittings Ltd. Colln. R. Quinnell

111 'Big chicken gate'
Mild steel tube and rod, hot formed, flame
metallized and painted. 2.5m high x 1.5m
long x 75cm depth of base. Colln. R. Quinnell

240

The White House Forge, Stanton-upon-Hine Heath, Shrewsbury, Salop, England

1935	born in Earley, near Reading, England apprenticed as a plumber, practising first in Australia then in England; then worked for the aircraft manufacturers Handley Page and for a government munitions factory
1964-70	trained with Bob Bridgeland, and on CoSIRA courses
1970	set up own workshop near Reading
1979	in partnership with Giuseppe Lund
1980-81	took part in limited competitions for designs for gates for St Paul's and V&A
1981	won Hampshire County Council limited competition for a pair of gates for Winchester Great Hall

Exhibitions
1980   Lindau

Public Collections
V&A

Exhibits

112* Staircase balustrade (photograph) 1980
Mild steel. Commissioned by Jock Thomas, Builder, Shrewsbury, for a house in Condover, Salop. Private Colln.

113 Candlestick 1980
Mild steel, forged, fire-welded and arc-welded. 38cm high x 68.5cm wide x 23cm deep. Colln. A. Robinson

114* Garden Lamp 1981
Mild steel and glass (hand-blown by George Elliott); forged by power hammer and arc-welded and painted. Approx 3m high x 1.5m wide. Colln. A. Robinson

115* Design for a pair of gates for Winchester Great Hall 1981
96.5cm high x 71cm wide (the actual gates approx 4.2m high x 7.2m wide). Commissioned, after a limited competition, by Hampshire County Council as a gift from the people of Hampshire to the Hall to commemorate the wedding of the Prince and Princess of Wales in July 1981. Colln. Hants County Council

116 Gate 1980
Mild steel forged by power hammer. 1.2m high x 1m wide. Colln. A. Robinson

117 Pendants 1981
Stainless steel, forged, ground and polished. Approx 8cm high each. Colln. A. Robinson

118* Flowers 1981
Mild steel forged with a power hammer, polished and waxed. Approx 75cm high each. Colln. A. Robinson

241

46 Marchmont Crescent, Edinburgh, Scotland

1947	born in Mufulira, Zambia
1965-68	Birmingham College of Art
1968	Ethel Cook Bequest and Leverhulme travelling scholarship
1968-71	Royal College of Art
1971	Melchett Award from British Steel Corporation and RCA Silver Medal for designs for jewellery in stainless steel
1971-78	taught part-time at Manchester Polytechnic teaches part-time at Edinburgh College of Art

Exhibitions

1973   *Schmuck 73 – Tendenzen* Schmuckmuseum, Pforzheim

1974   *Observer Jewellery Exhibition:* London, Cardiff, Bristol, Edinburgh

1975, 1980   *Loot* Goldsmiths' Hall

1980   *New Faces* British Crafts Centre, London

1982   *The Maker's Eye* Crafts Council, London

Publications

Body Jewellery: International perspectives, Donald J Willcox 1974

Public Collections

Goldsmiths' Company, London; Royal Scottish Museum; Stoke-on-Trent Museum

Exhibits

119* Neckpiece 1972
Stainless steel, photopierced and etched, hand finished and polished. The centre piece is interchangeable with the fastening. 17.1cm long x 11.2cm diam. Colln. A. Shillito

120* Neckpiece 1972
Stainless steel, photopierced and etched, hand finished and polished. The centre piece is interchangeable with the fastening. 17.1cm long x 11.2cm diam. Colln. A. Shillito

121* Buckle 1972
Stainless steel, photopierced and etched, hand finished and polished. 19.3cm long x 5.6cm wide. Colln. A. Shillito

---

Woodside Sneads Green, Nr. Droitwich, Hereford and Worcester, England

1930   born in England

1950-52   trained at Loughborough College

1955-56

1971   set up present workshop near Droitwich
Has taught for the last 20 years, latterly at Camberwell School of Art; has been wrought iron consultant to CoSIRA and now advises the Welsh Development Agency

Exhibitions

1973   *The Craftsman's Art* V&A & Crafts Council

1982   *The Maker's Eye* Crafts Council

Public Collections

Crafts Council

Exhibit

122* Bowl with serpentine handle 1976
Mild steel, hollowed under a power hammer, the handle scarfe-welded to the bowl. Diam 22.8cm x 10.1cm high. Colln. Crafts Council

---

4 Lower Road, Harmer Hill, Nr Shrewsbury, Salop

1957   born in England

1976-79   studied for BA in Wood/Metal/Ceramics/Plastic, specialising in jewellery, at Brighton Polytechnic

Exhibits

123 Curved pin 1980
Steel, blued, and inlaid with gold and silver. 12.3cm long. Colln. R. Stourton

124 Straight pin 1980
Steel, blued and inlaid with gold and silver. 13.4cm long. Colln. R. Stourton

125 Leaf-head pin 1980
Steel. 18.6cm long. Colln. R. Stourton

126* Pair of earrings 1980
Steel, inlaid with gold. 5.1cm long. Colln. R. Stourton

127 Brooch 1980
Steel. 7.2cm long. Colln. R. Stourton

Alison Varley   James Wallace

242

Peacock Cottages, Cawston, Norfolk,
England

1954	born in Brighton, England
1974-77	Brighton Polytechnic
1977-80	Royal College of Art
1980	Melchett Award, British Steel Corporation

Exhibitions

1980-81	*Loot* Goldsmiths' Hall
1981	*Ferrous metal jewellery* Arnolfini Gallery, Bristol
1981	*Black Jewellery* Oxford Gallery, Oxford

Exhibits

128 Pair of earrings 1980-81
Mild steel, inlaid with gold and silver. Max
width 2.6cm. Colln. A. Varley

129* Pill box 1980-81
Mild steel, pressed, inlaid with white, yellow
and green metals (silver and two-colour gold)
and oxidised black. Diam 5.5cm. Colln. A.
Varley

130* Hinged Box 1980-81
Mild steel, pressed and inlaid with white,
yellow and green metals, and the steel
oxidised black. 7.6cm long. Colln. A. Varley

---

374 West California, Memphis, Tennessee
38106, USA

1947	born in South Dakota, USA
1966	apprentice at Skunk Hollow Forge, Morrison, Colorado
1971	BA Western State College of Colorado, Gunnison, Colorado
1974-75	grants for research into damascus steel from Southern Illinois University
1977	Louis Tiffany Foundation grant
1977	MA Southern Illinois University, Carbondale, Illinois
since 1978	director, National Ornamental Metal Museum, Memphis, TN
1980	Fellowship, National Endowment for the Arts
1979-81	president ABANA

Exhibitions

1976	*Iron-Solid wrought USA* Southern Illinois University, Carbondale, ILL (and tour)
1978	*Blacksmiths 78* State University of New York, Purchase, NY
1980	*Southeastern Contemporary Metalsmithing* Southern Arts Federation Touring Exhibition
1980	*Iron and Wood* Louisville Art Centre, Louisville, KY Colony Square, Atlanta, GA

Publications

Contemporary Ironwork Dona Z Meilach
Crown Press 1976 (Co author of chapter on
damascus steel)

Exhibits

131* Sled 1981
Wood and mild steel. 23cm high x 1.17cm
long x 35cm wide. Colln. J. Wallace

132* Knives (2) 1980
Mild steel blades, damascened, each approx
3.5cm high x 25cm long x 2cm wide.
Collns.: No 1 Dr Parviz Sanjabi, Carbondale,
Ill; No 2 Matthew Wallace, Denver, Colorado

Klaus Walz   David Watkins

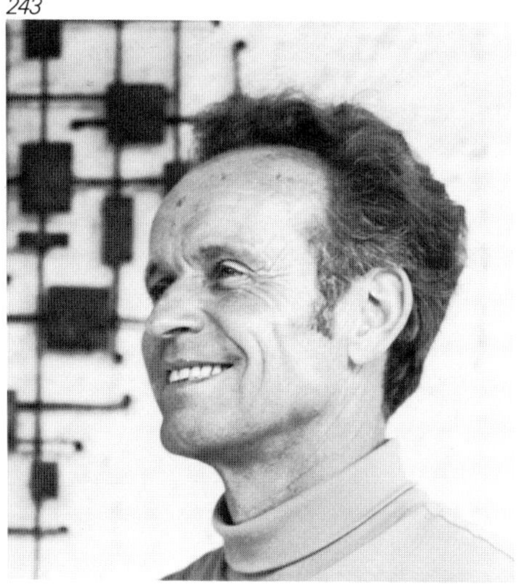

243

Arnikaweg 9, 7730 Villingen, West Germany

1924   born in Oberkirch, Germany
1947-48   apprentice locksmith
1948-50   worked with artist blacksmith
            Fromm at Schwenningen
1950-53   worked with artist blacksmith C.
            Wyland, Cologne
1953-54   attended the Meisterschule fur
            Kunsthandwerk in Munich, and
            took master's certificate
1954   set up own workshop in
            Villingen

Exhibitions
Lindau
1967   USA travelling exhibition of
            German crafts

Exhibit

133* Grille 1980
Mild steel. 2.30m high x 1.20m wide. Colln.
K. Walz

244

84 Cromwell Avenue, London N6, England

1940	born in Wolverhampton, England
1959-63	studied sculpture at Reading University and started working as a jeweller
1978	artist in residence, Western Australian Institute of Technology
1981	took part in limited competition for V&A gates commission and spent some weeks working in Al Paley's workshop in New York State

Exhibitions
Numerous one-man shows

1974	*Seven Golden Years* Goldsmiths' Hall *British Design* Philadelphia Museum of Art
1975	*Jewellery in Europe* Scottish Arts Council tour
1982	*The Maker's Eye* Crafts Council

Public Collections
Goldsmiths' Company, London; Crafts Council; Bristol City Art Gallery; Royal Scottish Museum; Kendal Museum; Science Museum; Vienna Museum for Angewandte Kunst

Publications
Architectural Review no 7, 1976; May 1979 *Crafts Magazine*
The World of the Makers, Edward Lucie-Smith
Contemporary Jewellery: a critical Assessment 1974-75 Ralph Turner

Exhibits

134 Hoop necklace 1979
Mild steel, forged and inlaid with steel and gold. 13.5cm approx diam. Private Colln.

135* Design for gates to V&A Ironwork Gallery 1981
Pencil and red crayon. 57cm high x 77cm wide. Submission to the limited competition held by the V&A and the DoE. Colln. D. Watkins

136* Design for a chandelier for the V&A Silvery Gallery 1982
Pencil and crayon. Approx 42cm wide x 19cm high. Colln. D. Watkins

137 Four suspended structures 1981
Mild steel, partly coloured. Approx 76cm square x 5.1cm high. Colln. D. Watkins

138* Plant stand with twists 1981
Mild steel. 29.5cm high x 66cm diam. Coll. D. Watkins

139* Bangle 1979
Mild steel, inlaid with gold. Diam 8.3cm. Colln. V&A Museum no M56-1981

140* Neckpiece 1980
Mild steel wire, coated with neoprene. 13.5cm approx diam. Colln. D. Watkins

245

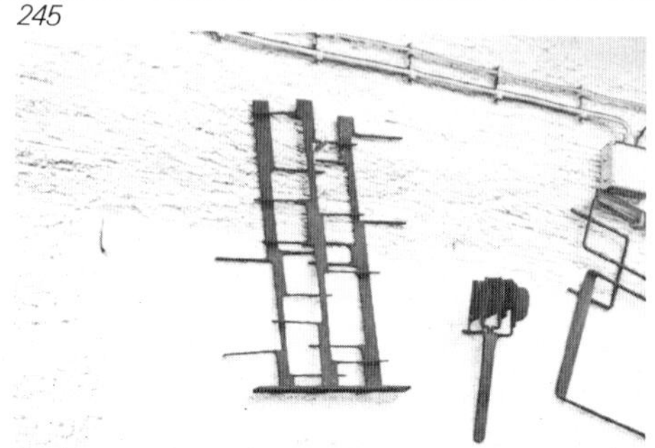

c/o W. A. Wootton, 2 Quineys Road, Shottery, Stratford-on-Avon, Warwickshire, England

1952	born in Torquay, England
1974-76	course in constructural design at St. Paul's College of Education, Cheltenham
1976-78	employed in general fabrication and smithing
1979	part-time study with Alan Knight
1979-80	apprentice with Paul Zimmermann, Pliezshausen, W. Germany
1980-82	apprentice with the firm of Manfred Bergmeister, Ebersberg, W. Germany
1981	journeyman's certificate (Gesellenprüfung-Schlosser-Handwerk) from Metall-Innung, Munich

Exhibitions
1980 Lindau

Exhibits

141* Candlestick 1980
Mild steel, forged from flat plate finished with hot wax. Made in Zimmermann's workshop. 34cm high x 19cm wide x 19cm deep. Colln. Paul Zimmermann

142* Candleholder 1980
Mild steel, forged from flat plate, finished with hot wax. Made in Zimmermann's workshop. 7.5cm high x 8.5cm wide x 11cm deep. Colln. A. Wootton

143* Fire-grate 1981
Mild steel, finished by hot-waxing. 21cm high x 45cm wide x 38cm deep. Commissioned by the Crafts Council for this exhibition. Colln. A. Wootton

144* Altar cross 1980
Mild steel, forged from flat plate, finished by hot-waxing. 84cm high x 15cm wide x 58cm deep. Colln. A. Wootton

145* Doorknocker 1980
Mild steel, finished by hot-waxing. 1.3cm long x 7.5cm approx max. wide. Colln. A. Wootton

246

Atelier Zimmermann, Kronengasse 6, Postfach 1, 7401 Pliezshausen, West Germany

1939	born in Tübingen
1953-56	apprentice metalworker
1956-60	won award for gifted students and spent time in intermediate study, partly abroad
1962	qualified as master craftsman after a year at Luisenschule, Munich
1962-63	taught in vocational institute in Munich
1964	set up own workshop in Pliezshausen
1975-82	part-time teaching in blacksmithing at Technical School in Tübingen

Exhibitions
since **1960** frequent exhibitions in Germany and some abroad
1965, 69, 74 and **80** Lindau

Exhibits

146* Grille 1980
Mild steel. 1.85cm high x 75cm wide x 8cm deep. Colln. P. Zimmermann

147* Candleholder no 2 1980
Mild steel. 10cm high x 17cm wide x 9cm deep. Colln. P. Zimmermann

148* Candleholder no 3 1980
Mild steel. 8cm high x 18cm long x 12cm deep. Colln. P. Zimmermann

149* Candleholder no 4 1980
Mild steel. 10cm high x 31cm long x deep. Colln. P. Zimmermann

Lighting

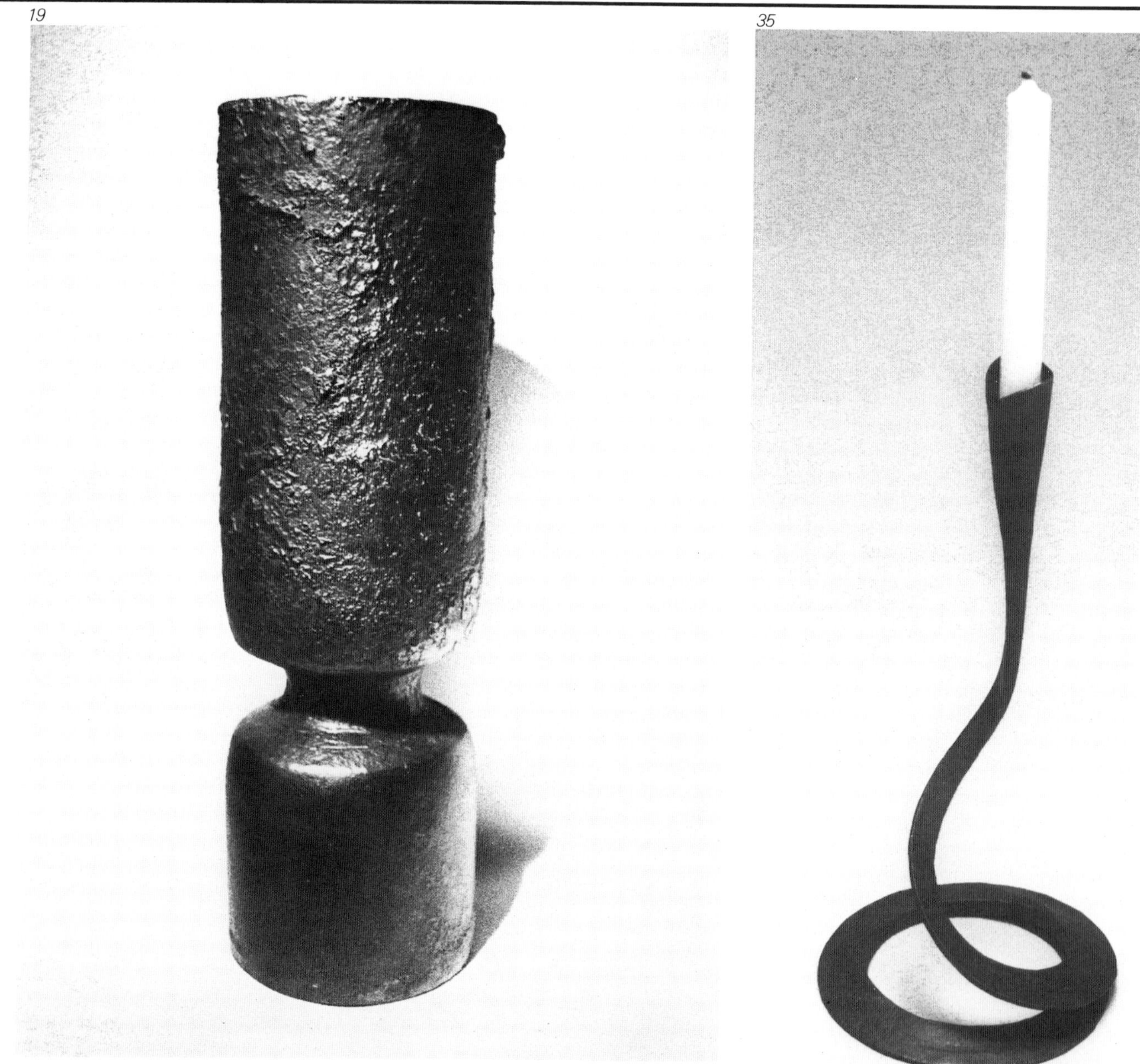

100
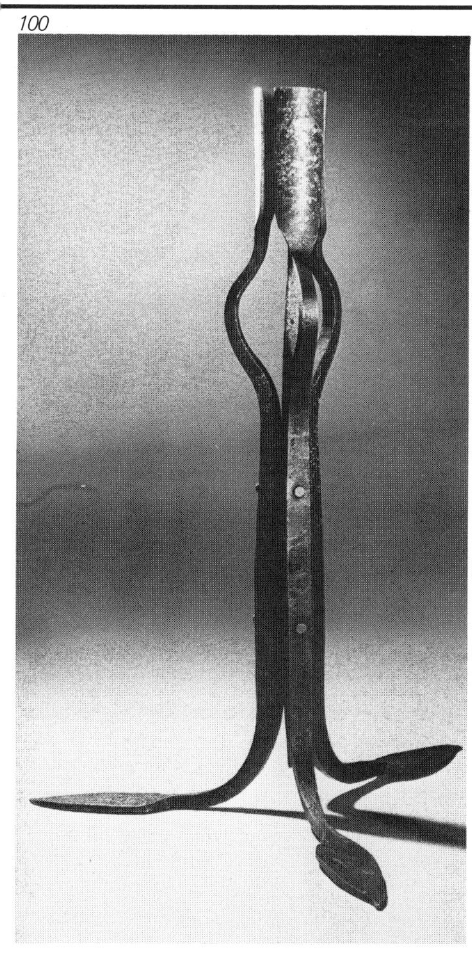

114
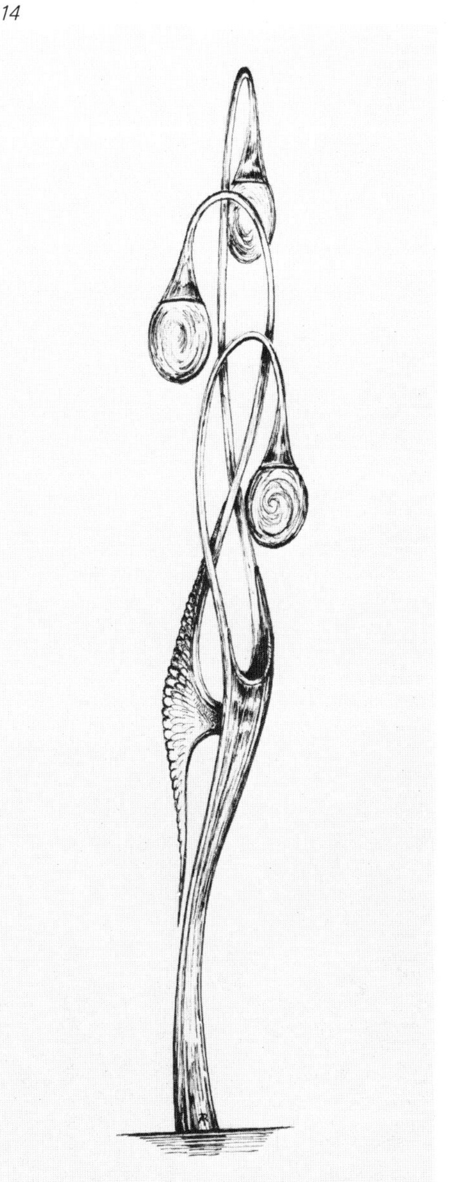

141

149

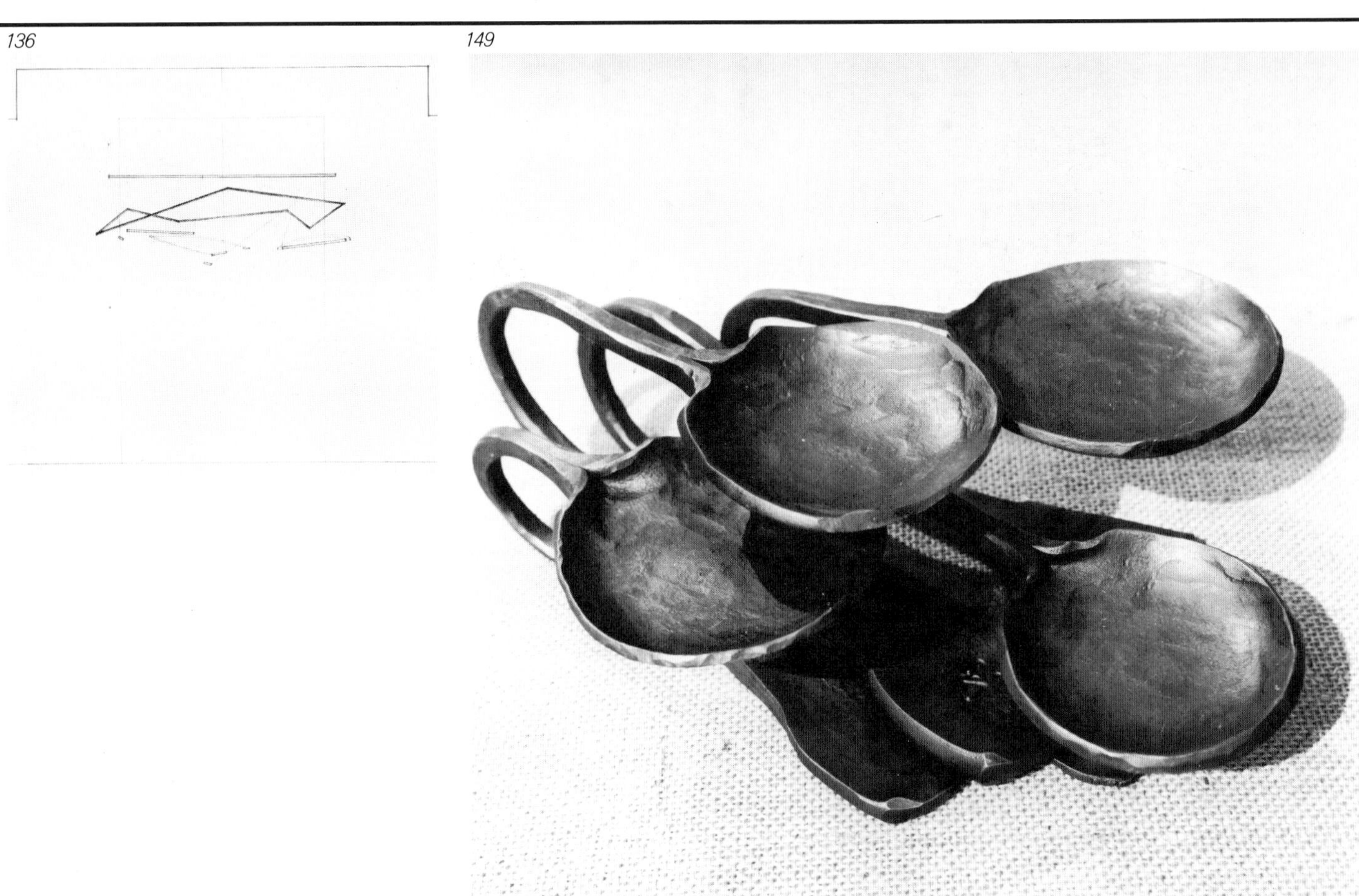

147

32
33
38

39

50

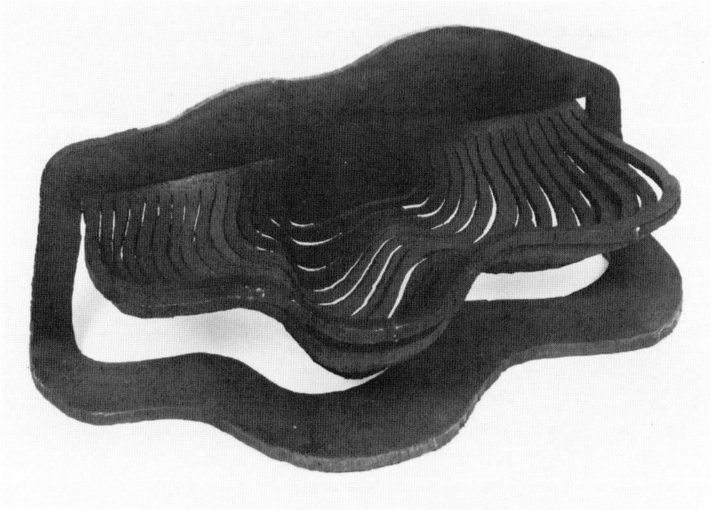

51

57
82
80
94

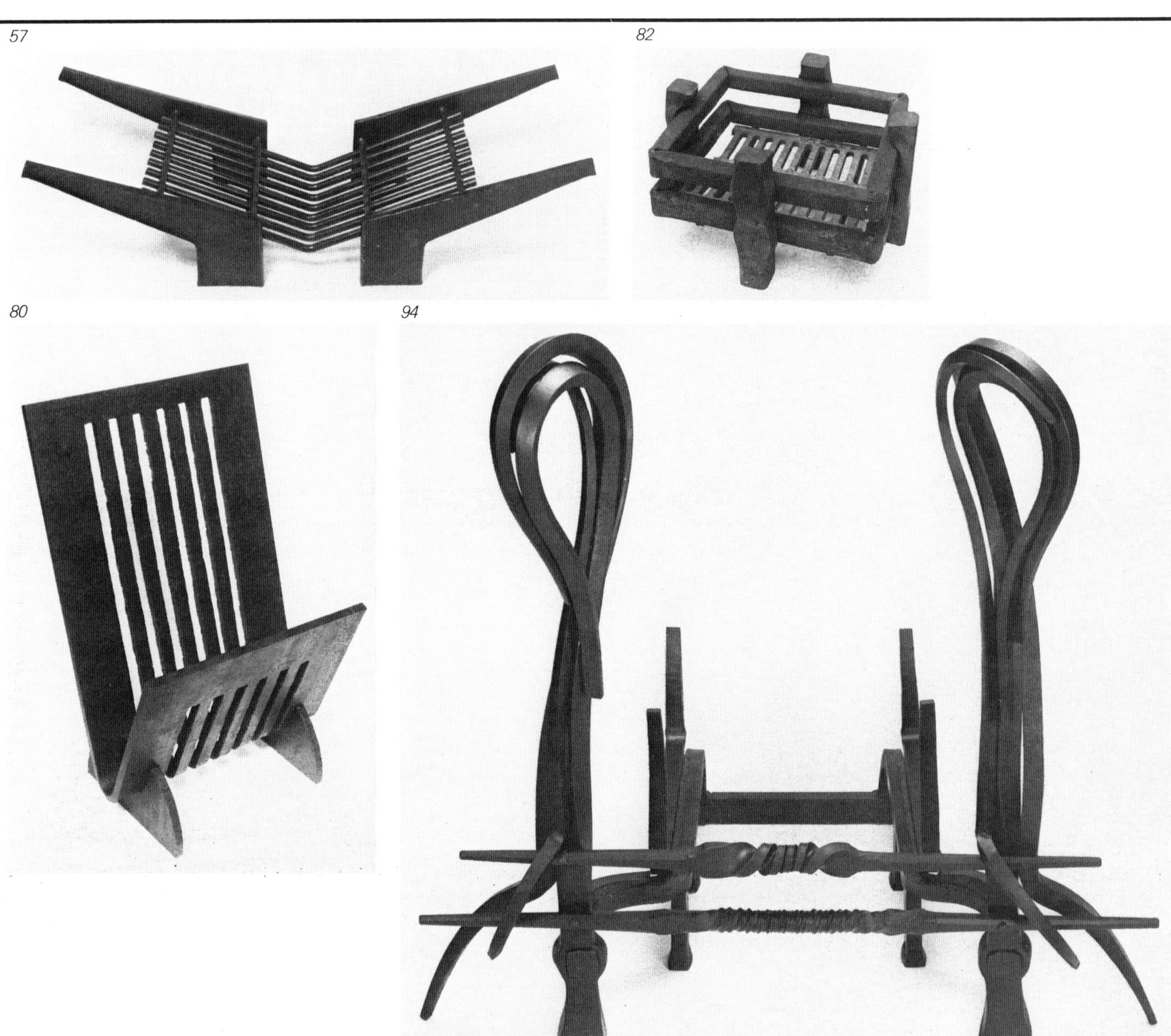

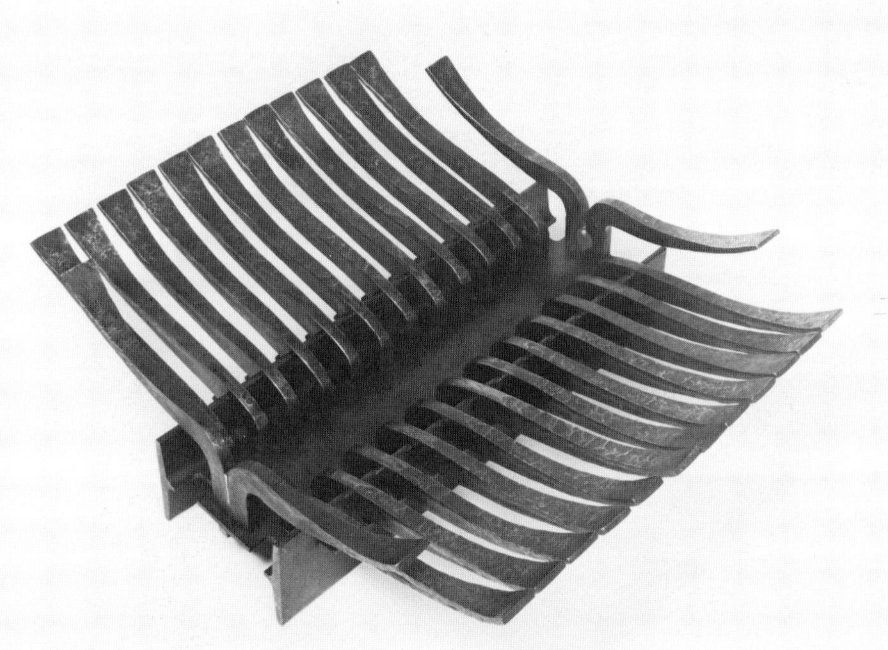

107

143

Ecclesiastical items

144

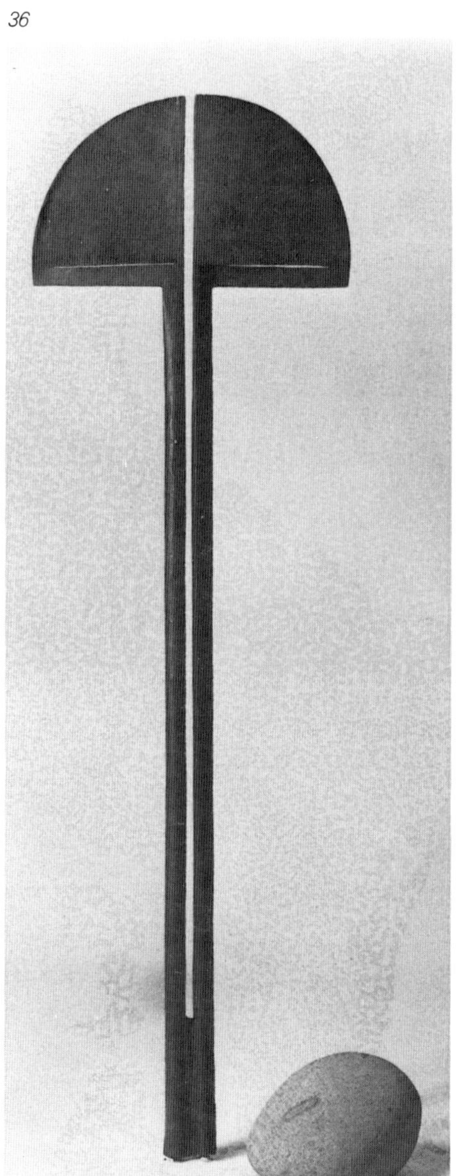

36

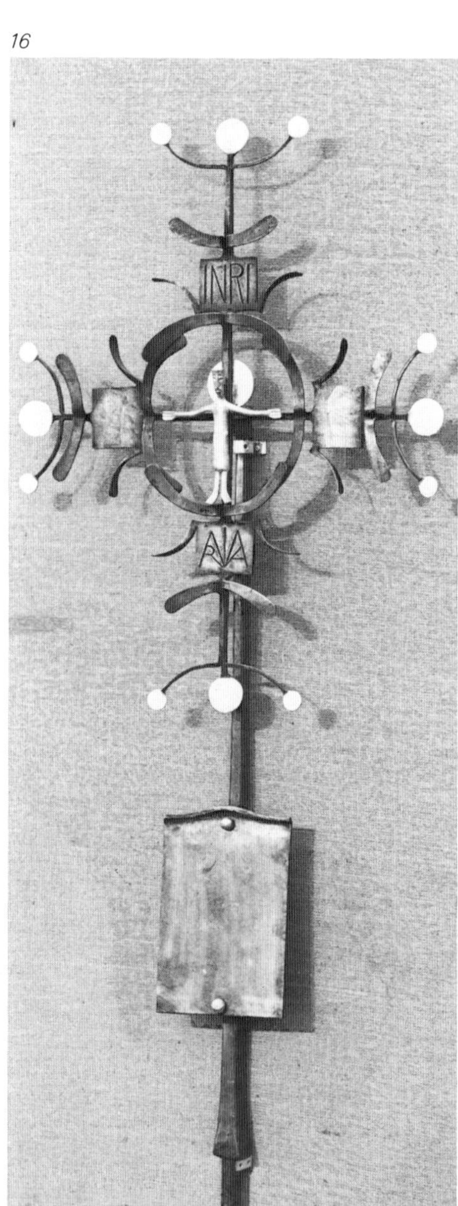

16

132

9

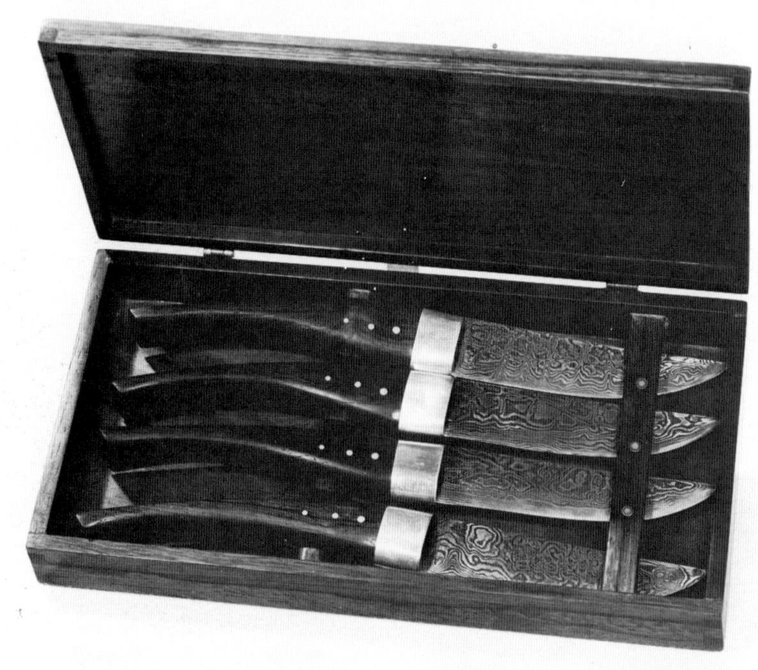

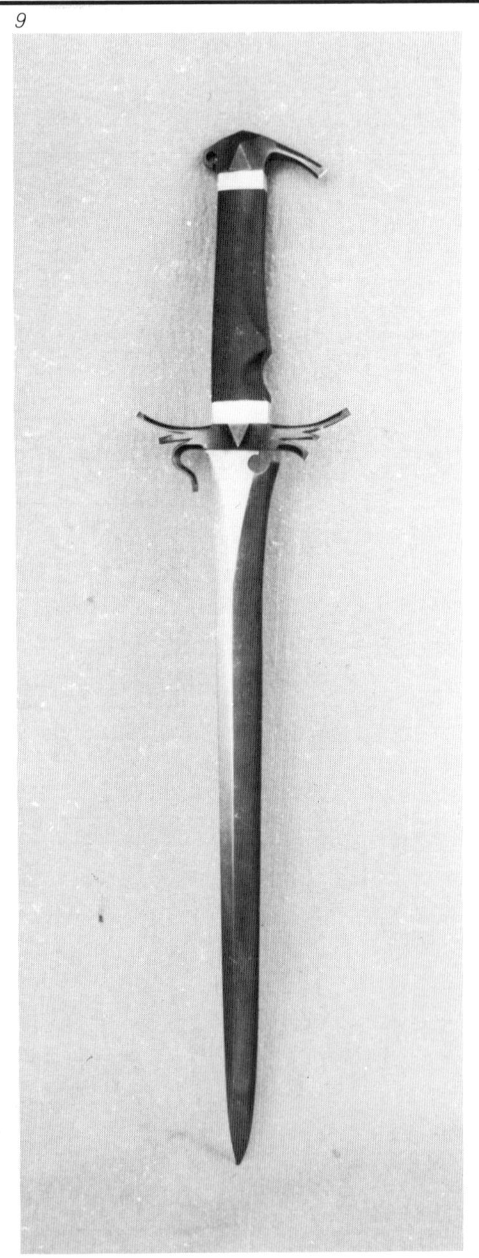

1

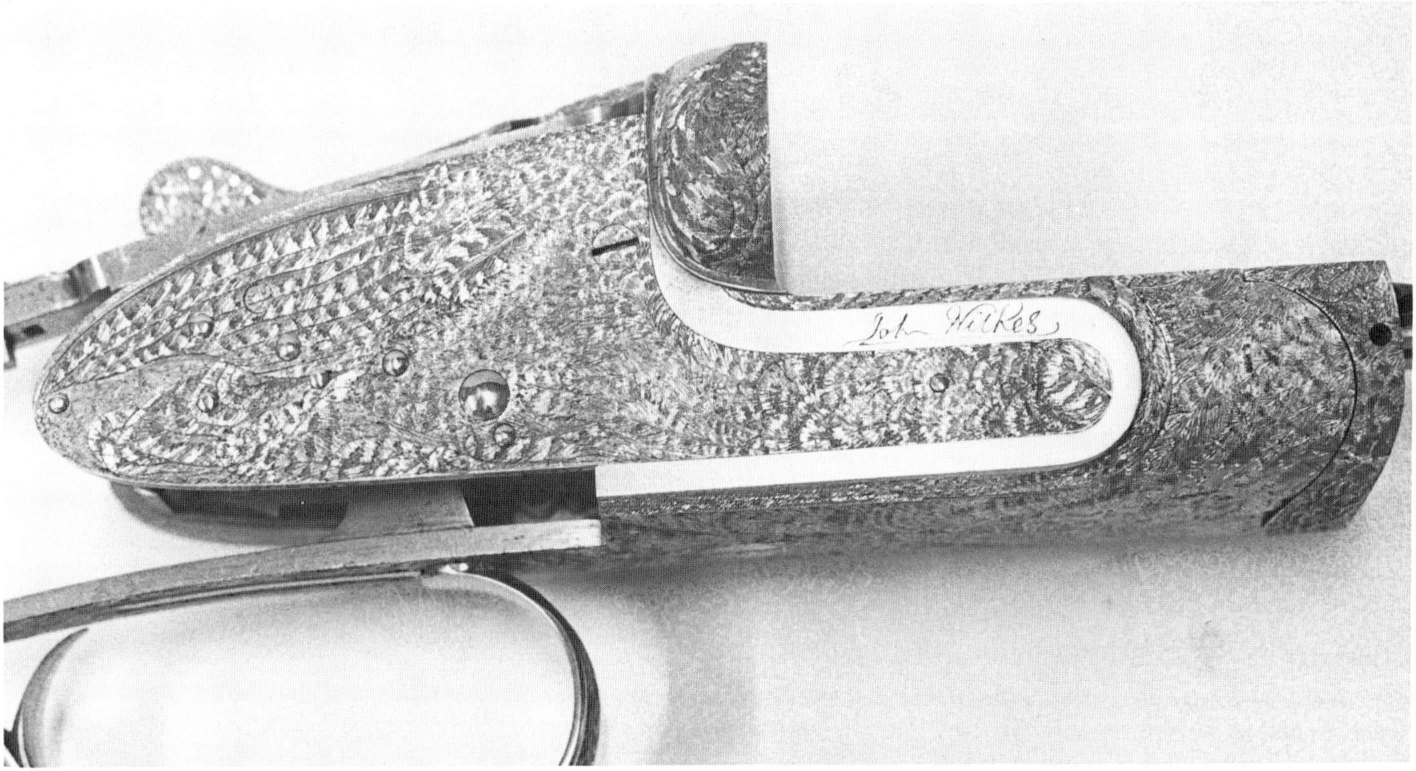

131

13

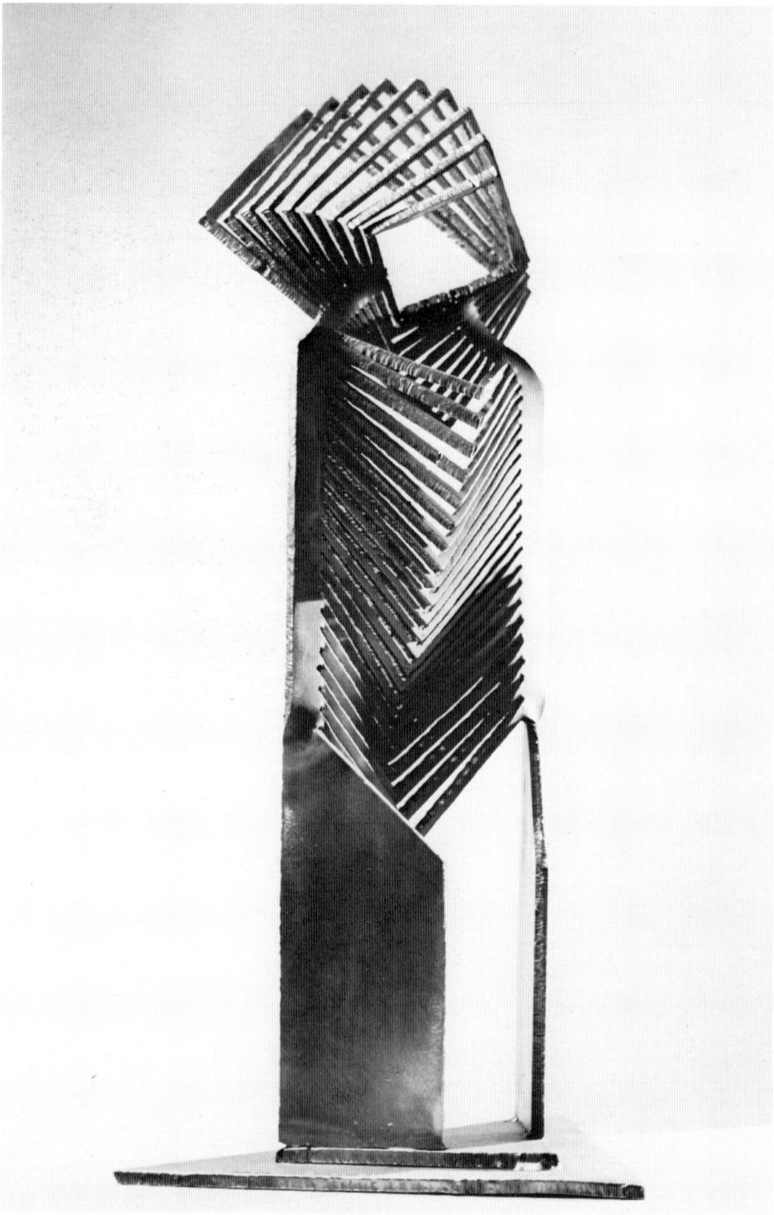

14

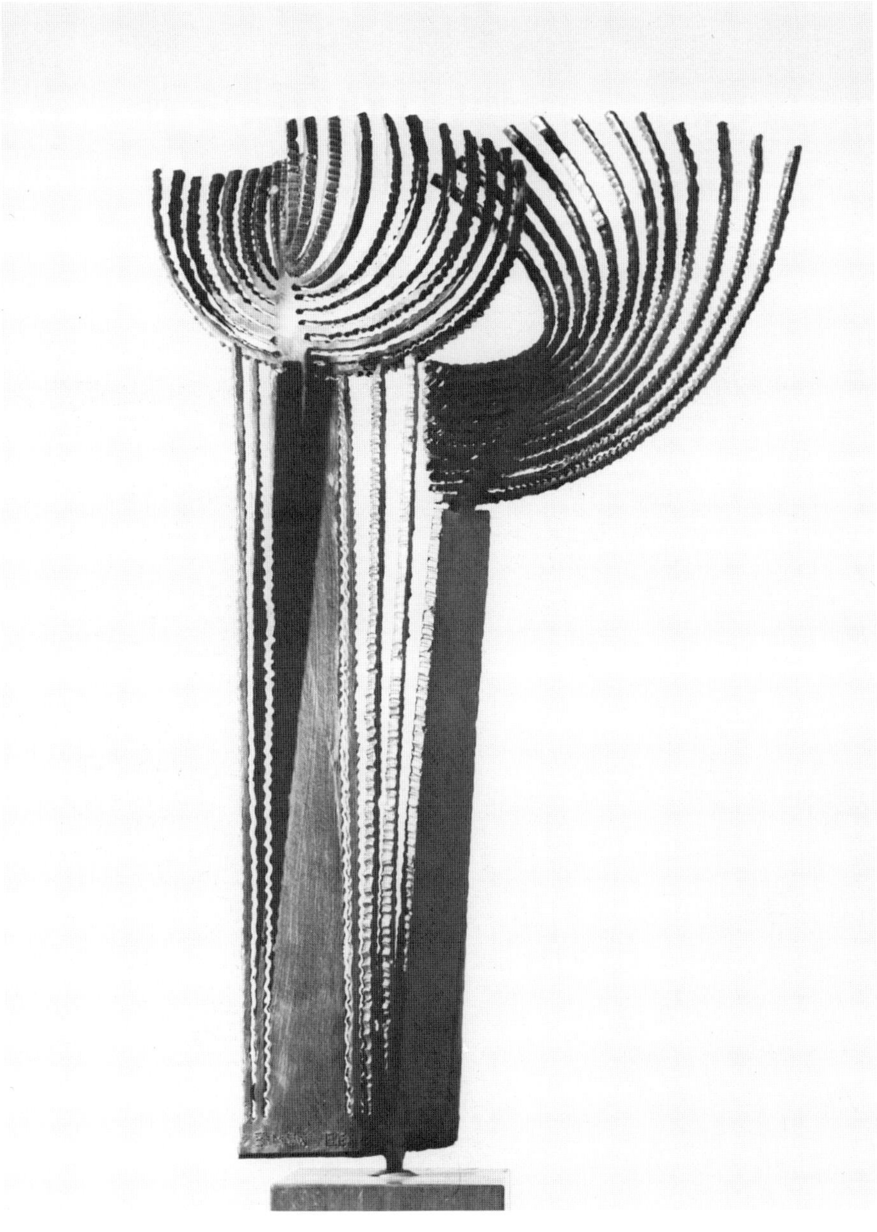

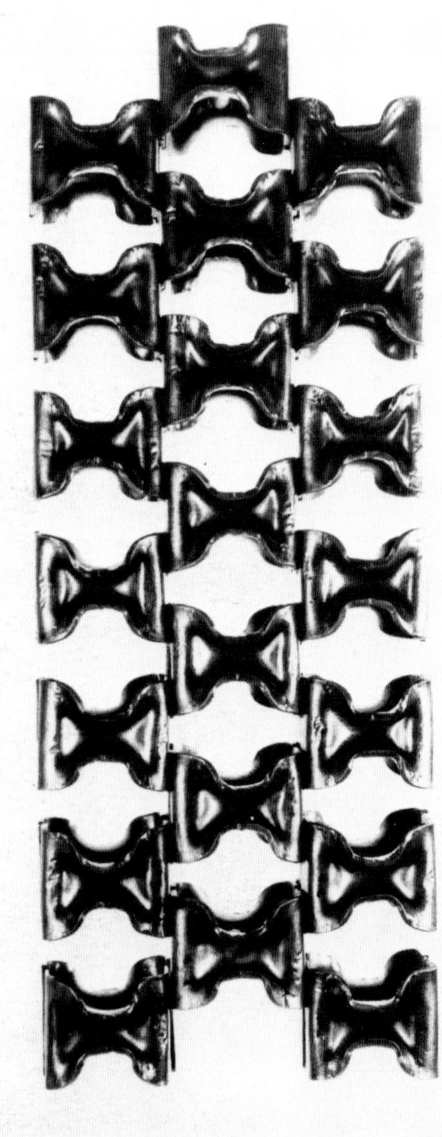

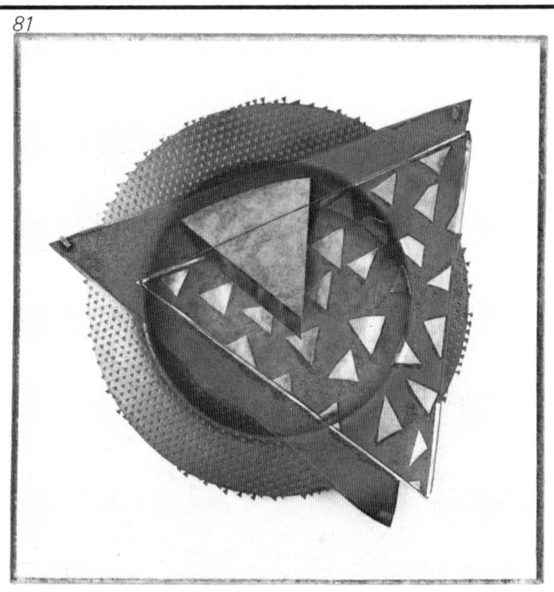

81

118

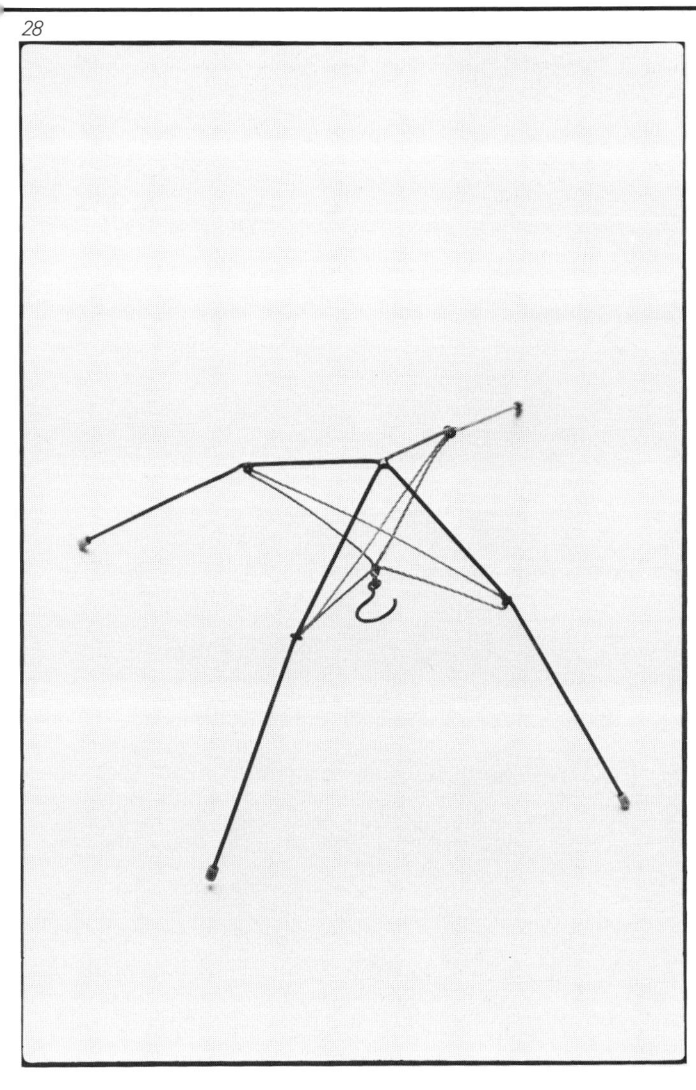

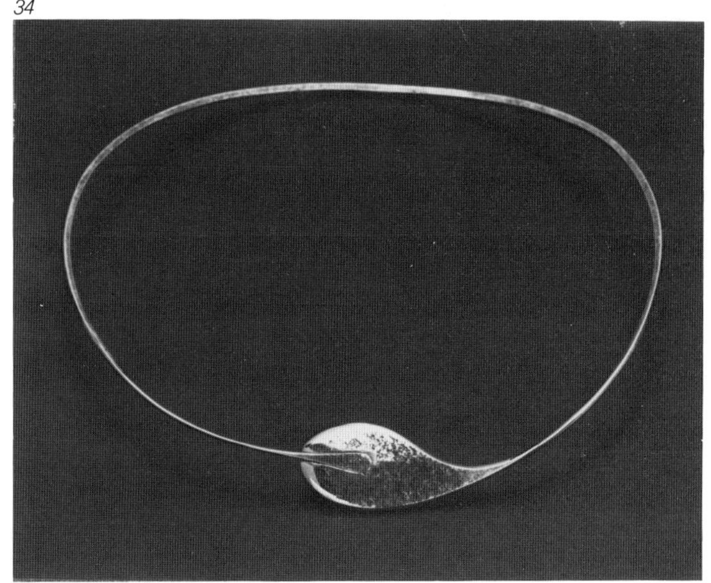

34

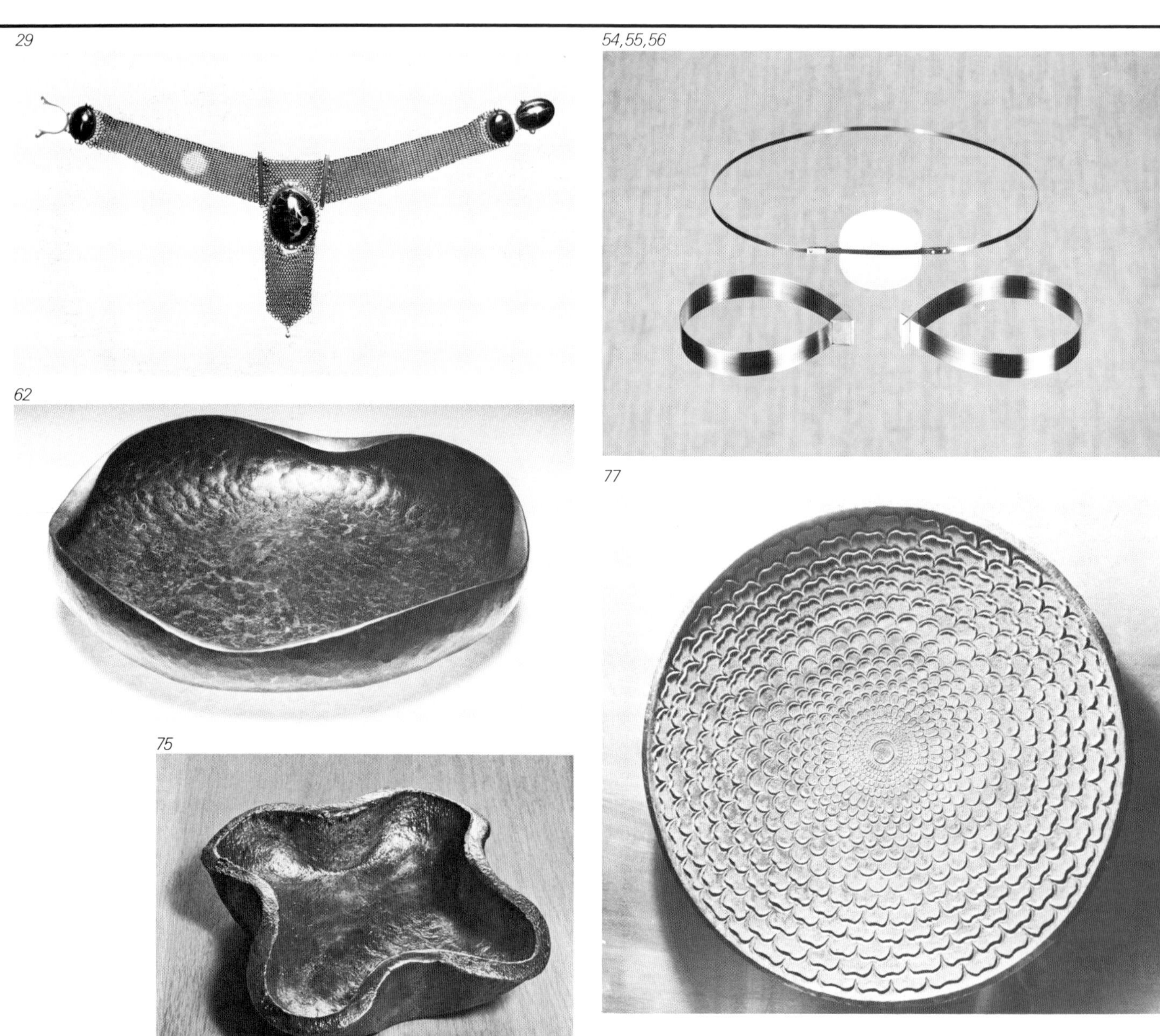
29
54,55,56
62
77
75
80

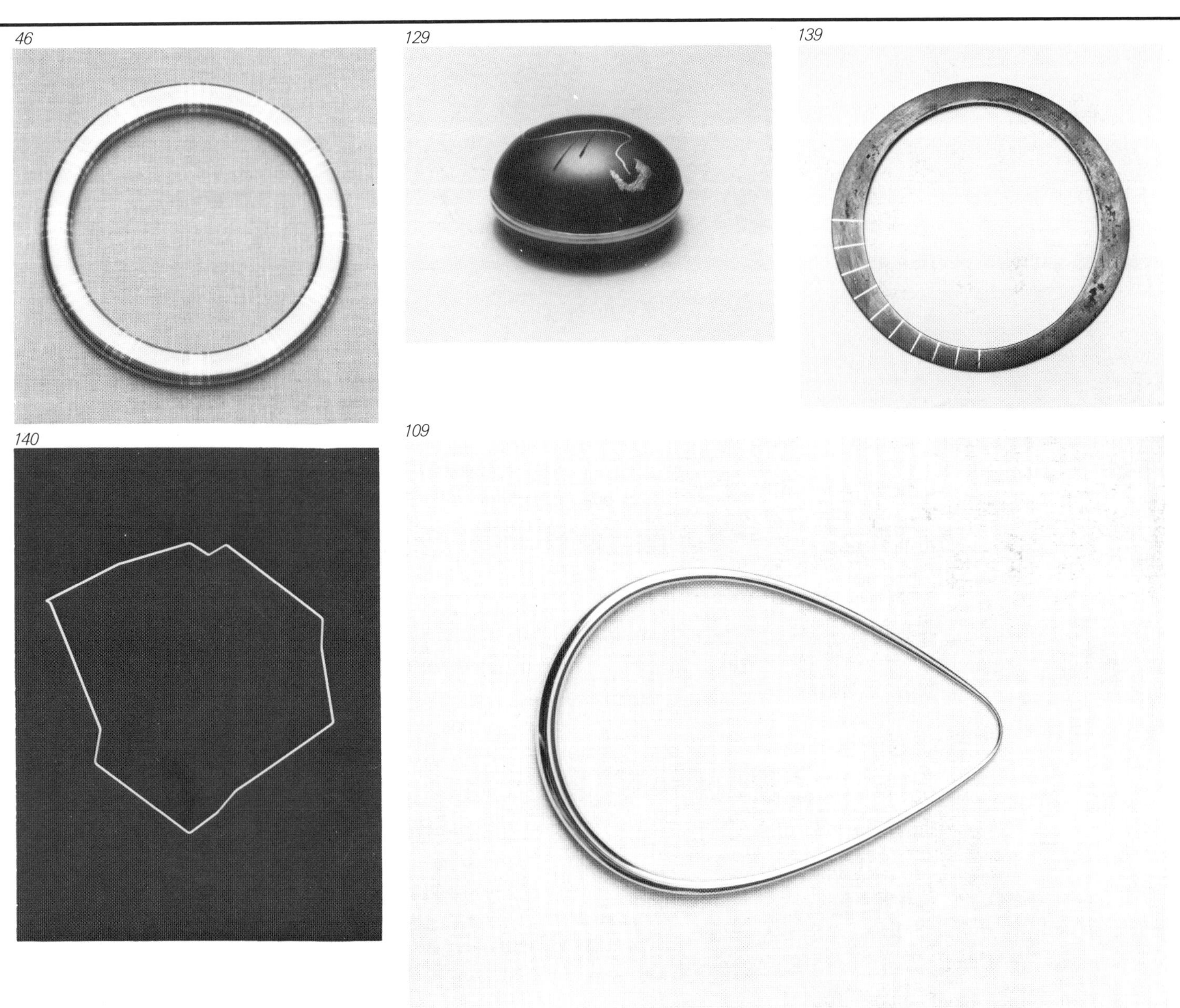

46
129
139
140
109

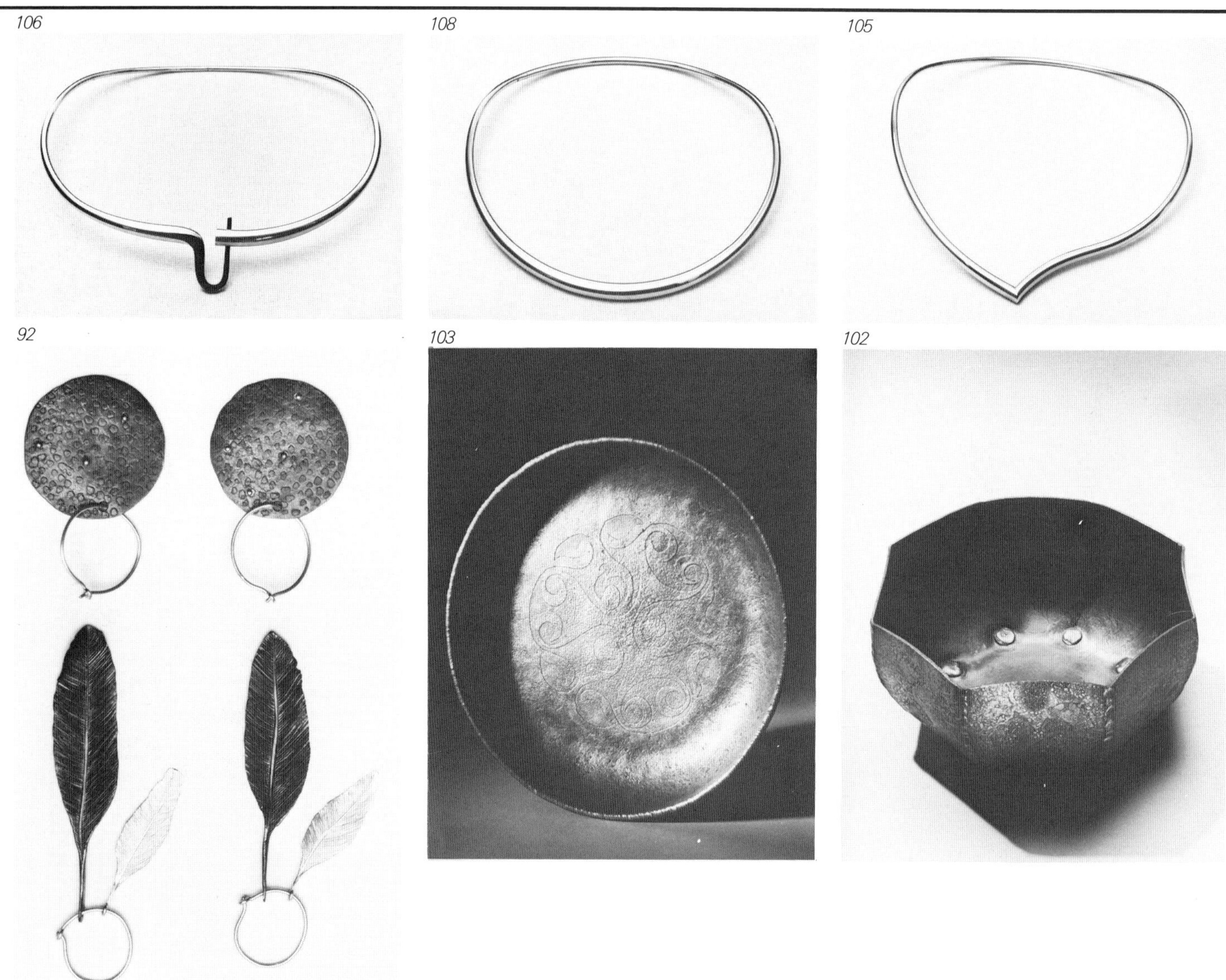

106
108
105
92
103
102
91

126
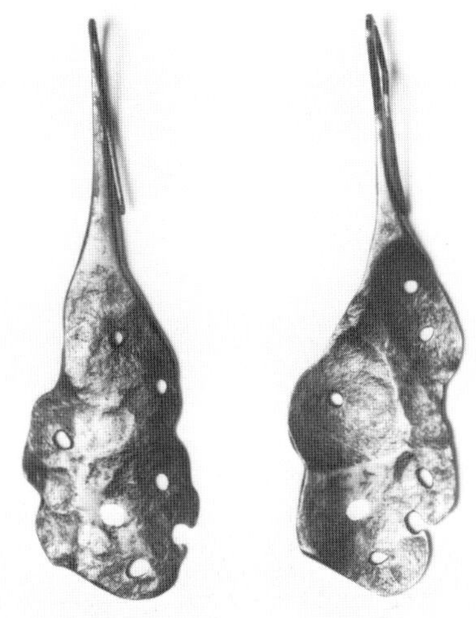

121
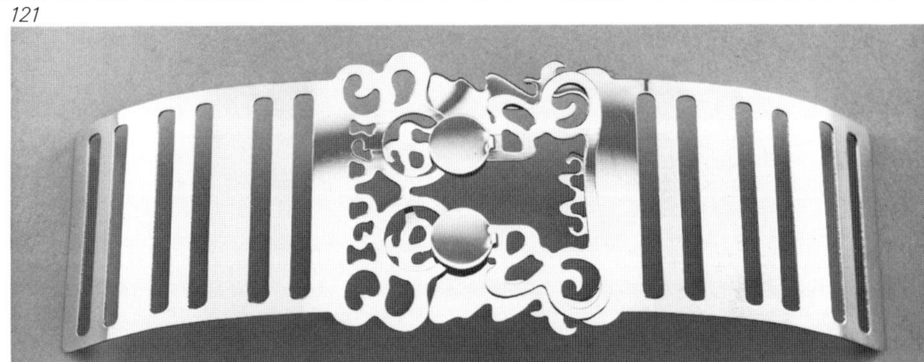

119,120
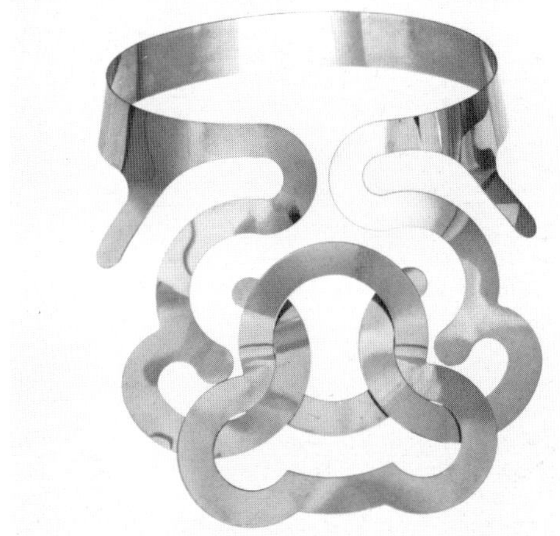

130
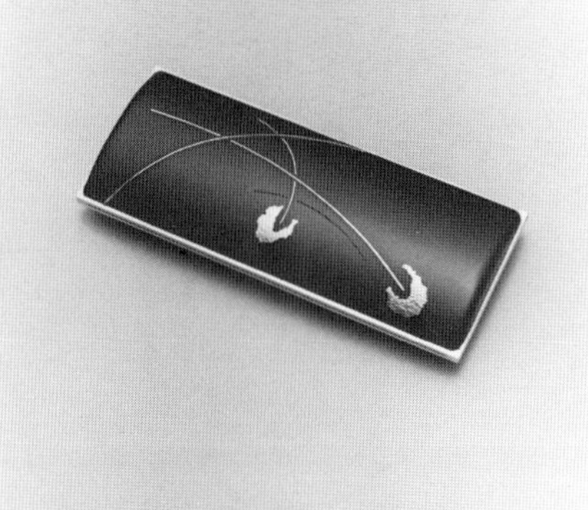

122

24

31

- FURNITURE -
WROUGHT IRON STAND
DESIGNED BY   DRAWN BY   DATE   SCALE
J. DITTMEIER   J. DITTMEIER   JAN 1981   AS NOTED
ACTUAL SIZE
© JOHN M. DITTMEIER, DOVER, DELAWARE, USA, 1981

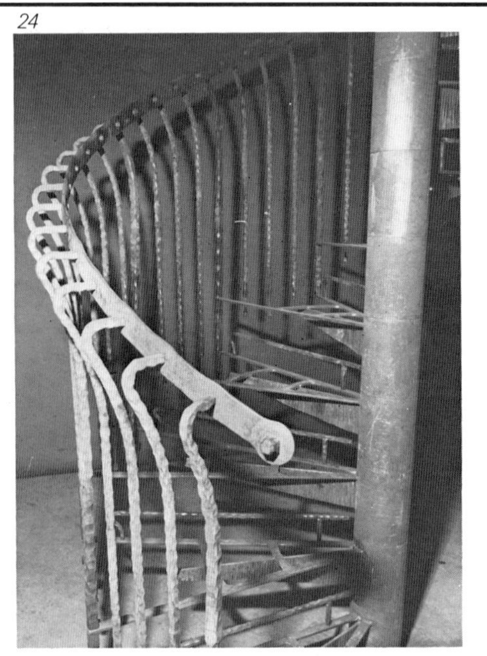

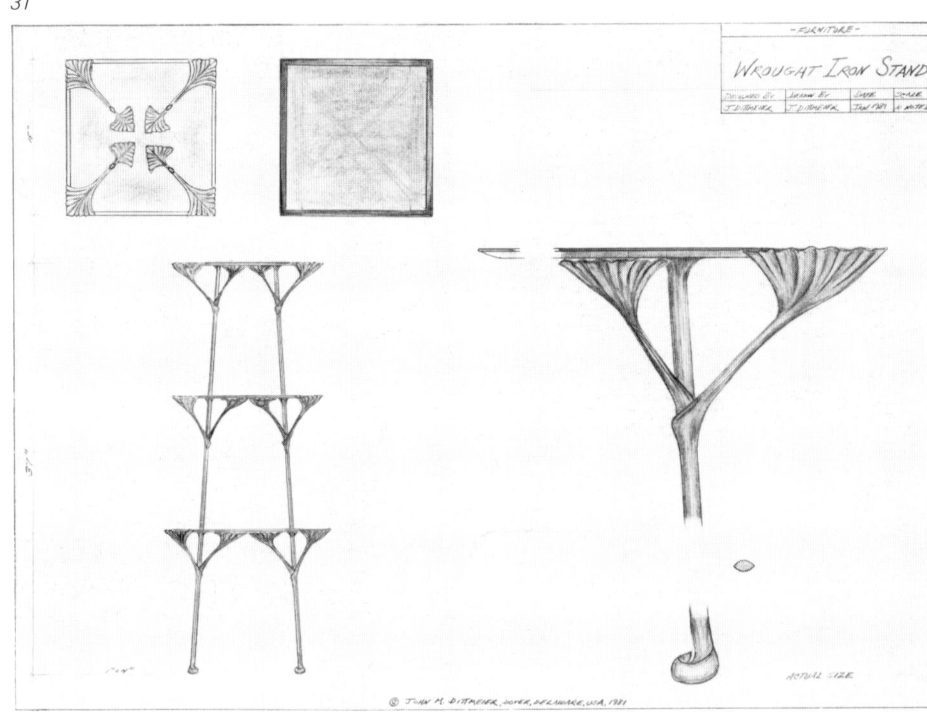

21

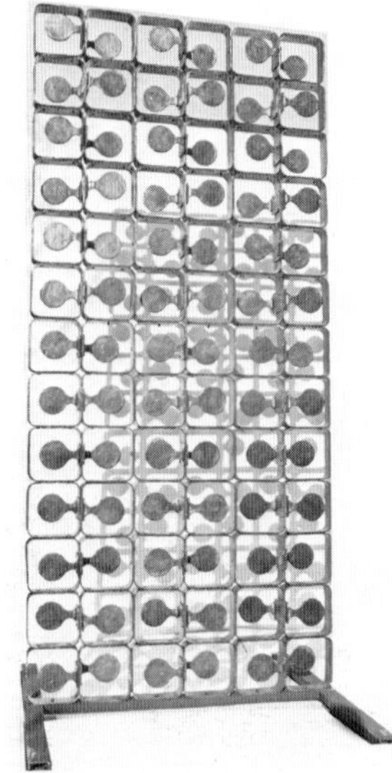

44

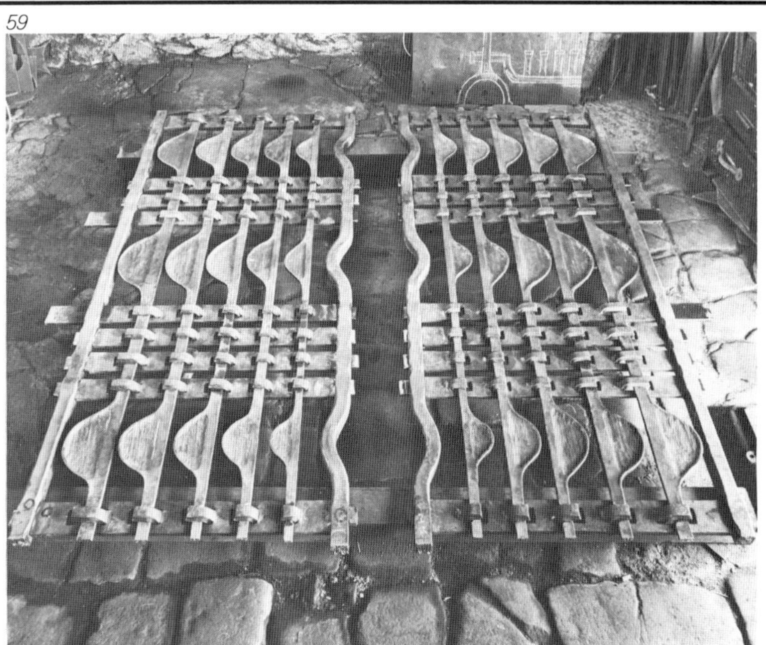

59

68

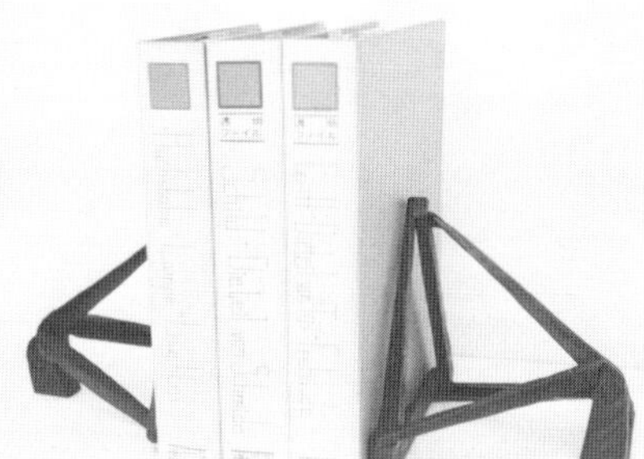

69

70

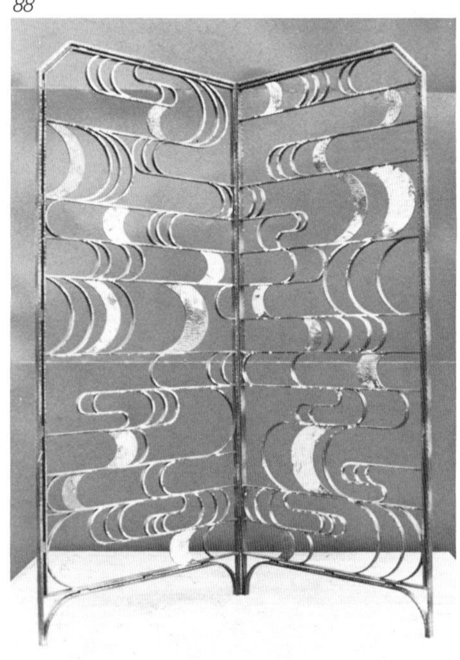

135

133

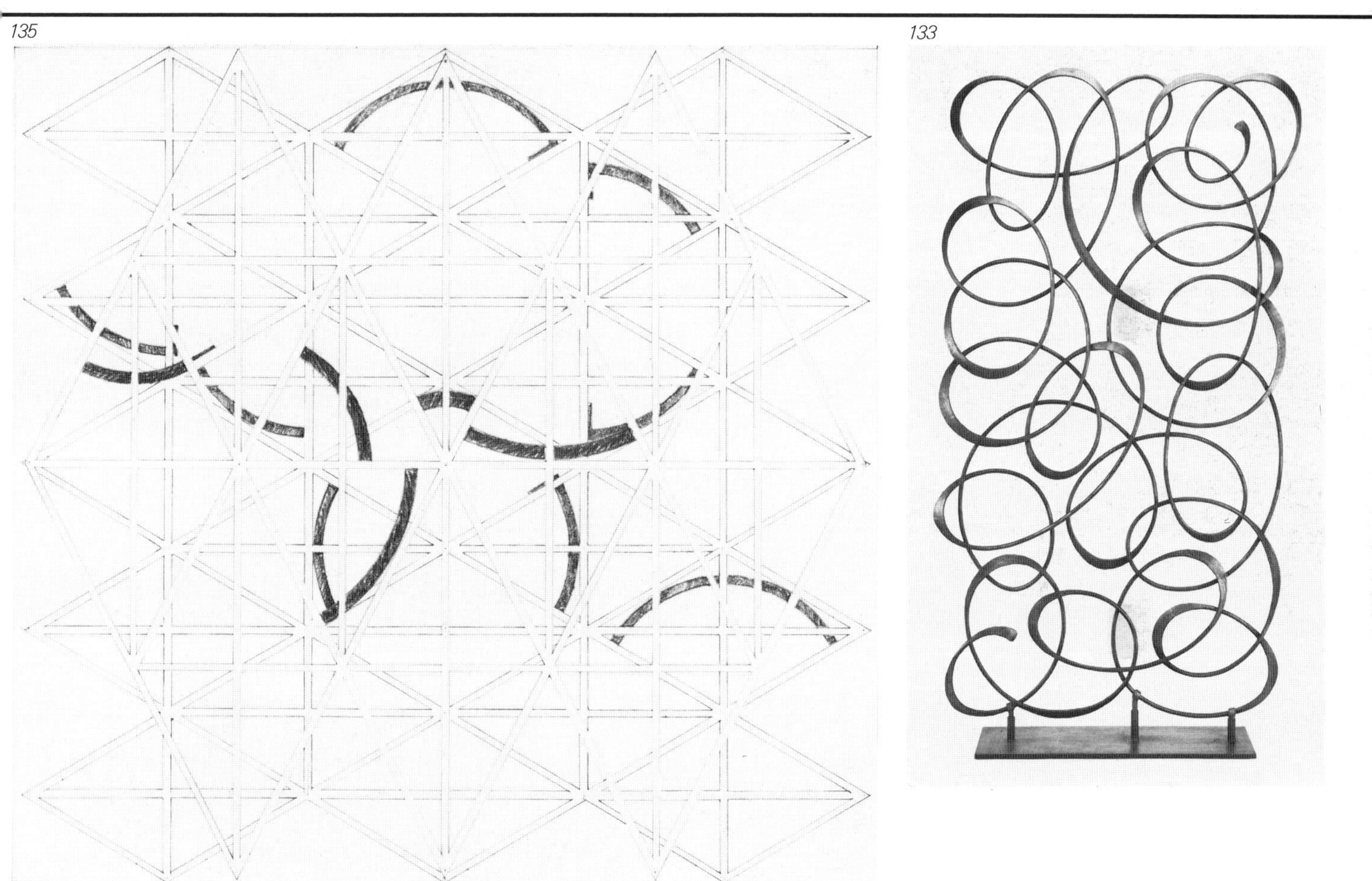

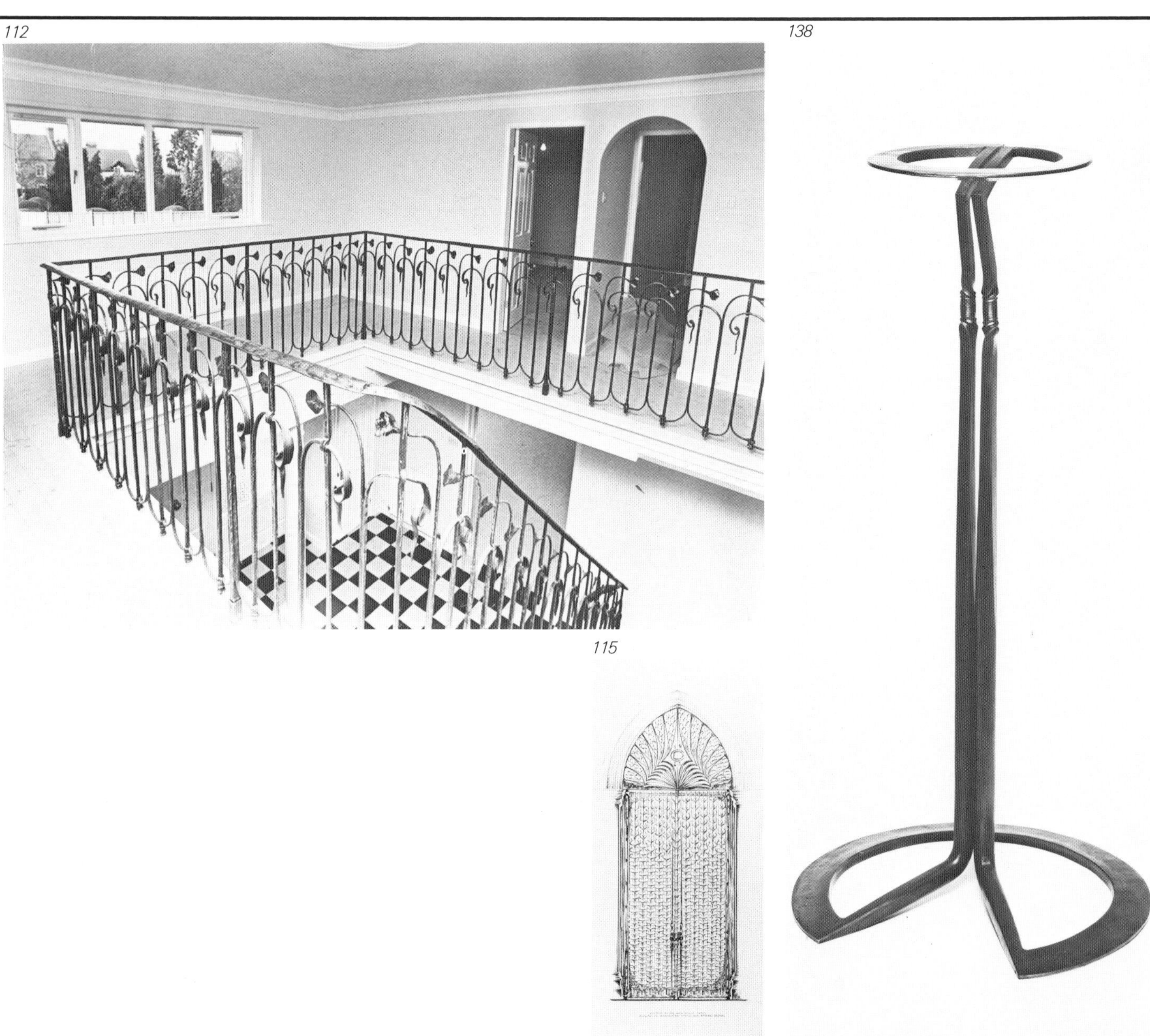

112

138

115

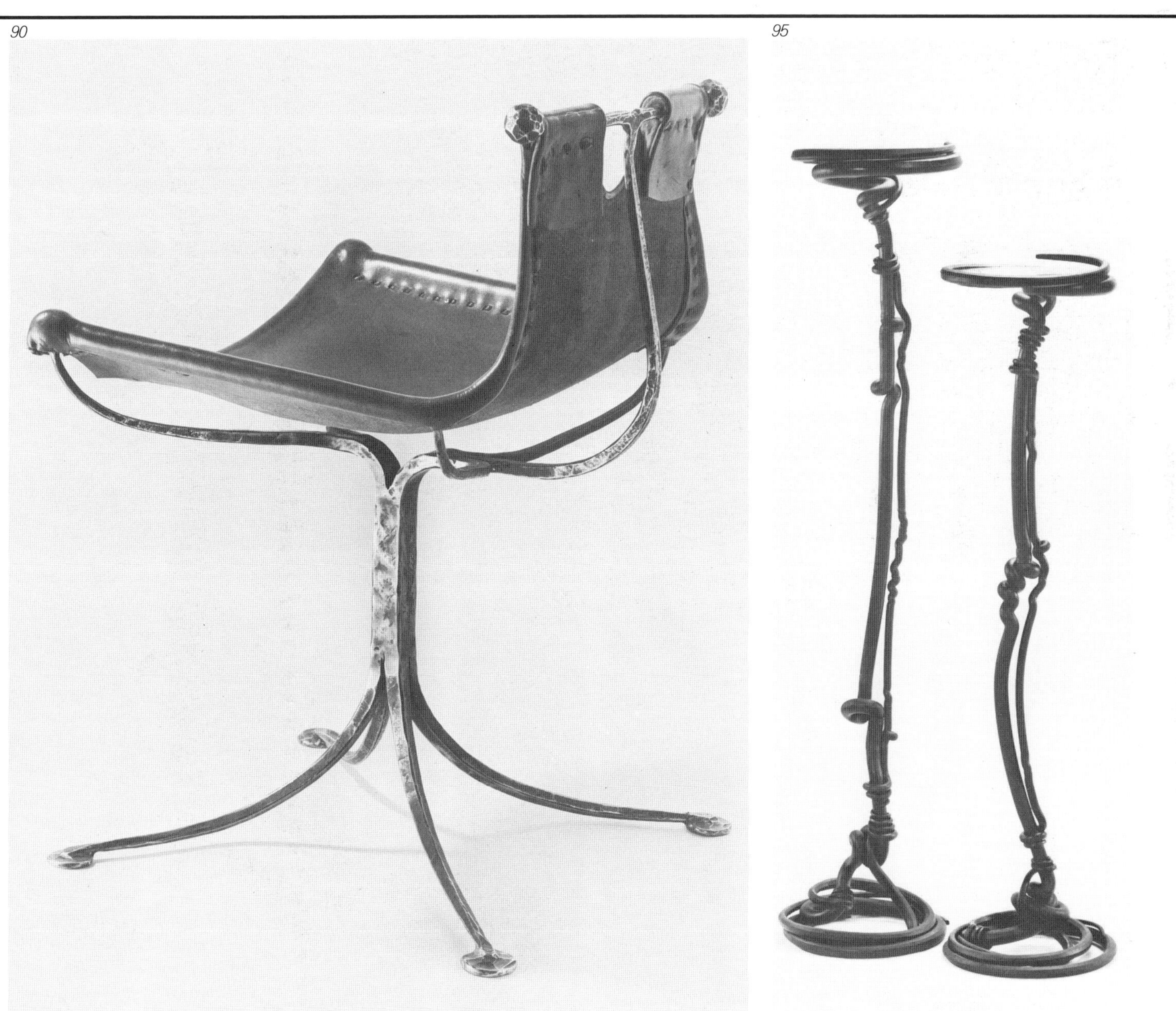

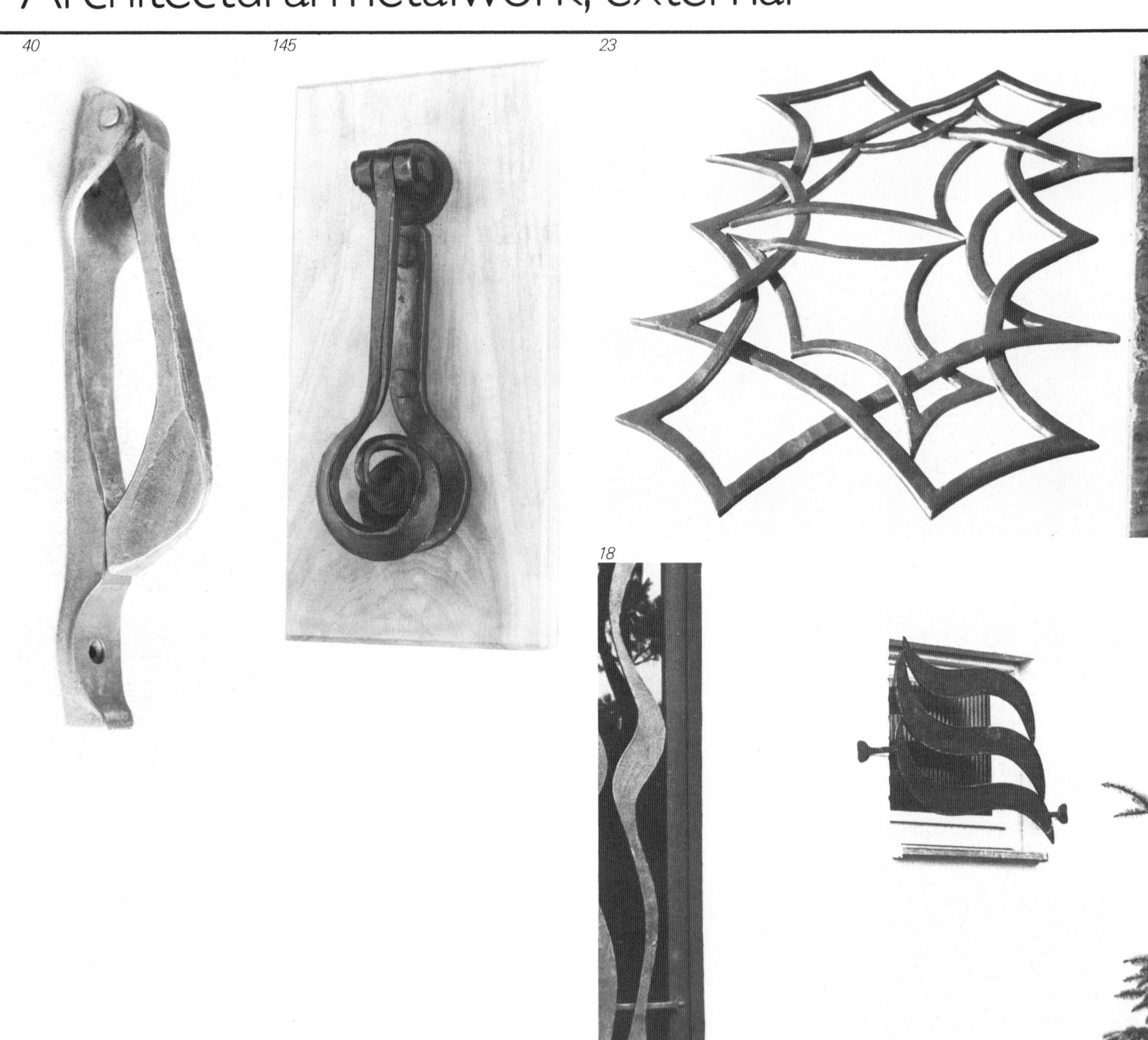

301

83

43

53

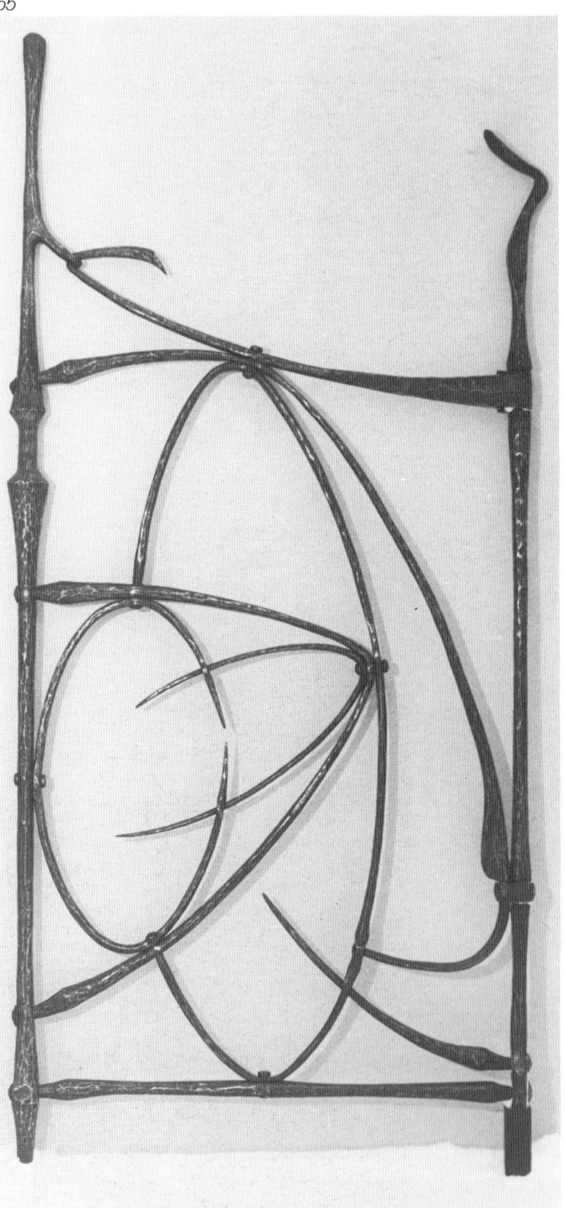

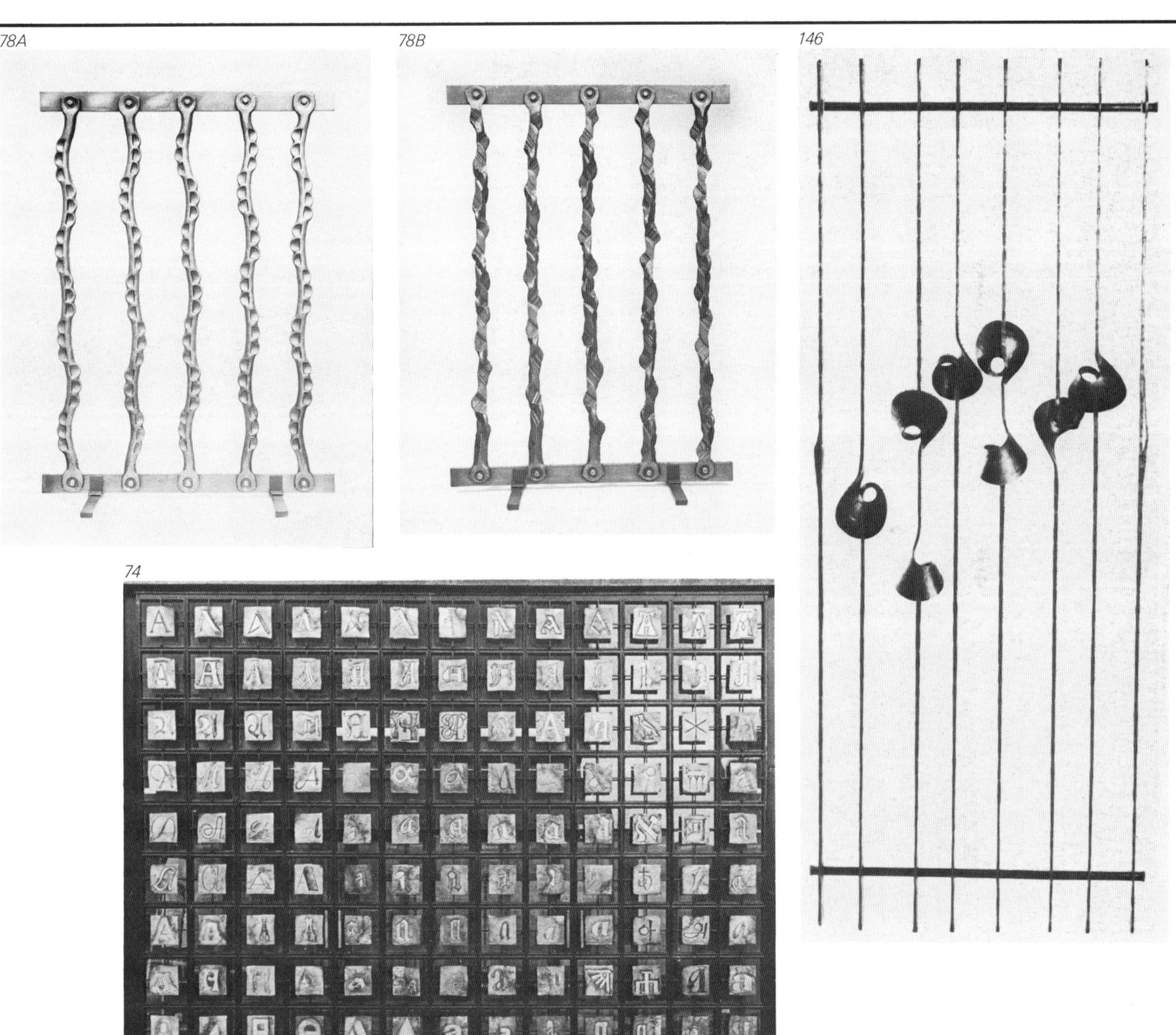

78A
78B
146
74

15

89

58

84

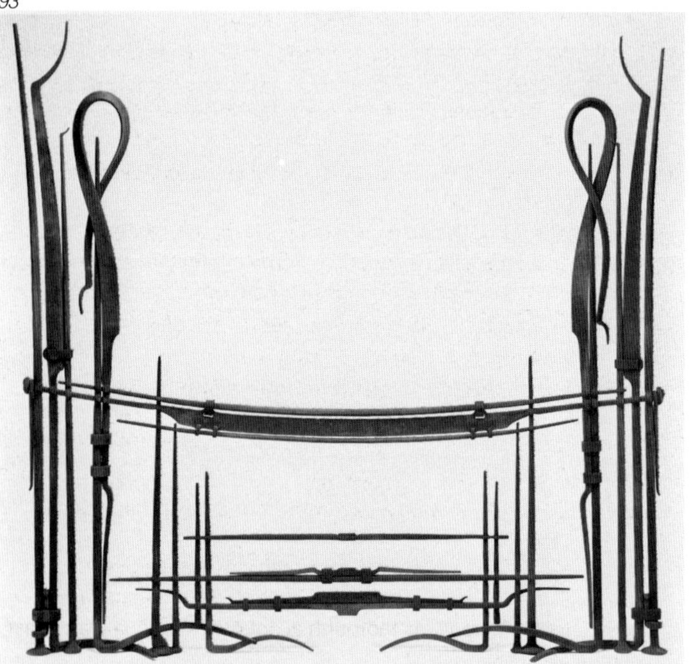

Photographic credits
Photographs have kindly been provided by the lenders to the exhibition and by the following:
Carla Arnold, Dan Bailey, Ian Dobbie, John Eagle, Foto d'arte Treviso G. Fili, Daniel Germann Fotostudio, Gordon Hammonds Photography Company, Hunter Museum of Art, Fred Hugel, Elmar Ludwig, Richard Margolis, Barbara Meffert, Foto Poldi, Graham Portlock, Josef Ptacek, Urpo Rouhiainen, David Ramsey, Dudley Reed, Riedel Photostudio, Fotostudio Schiller, G. Schumacher, Brian Young.

96

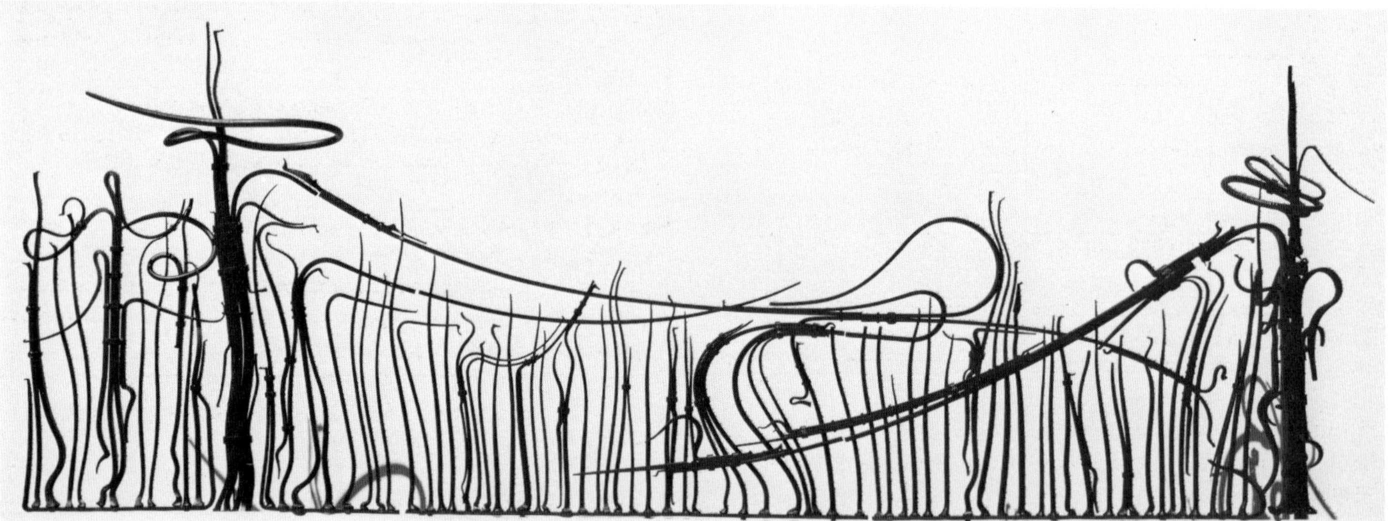

Bibliography

This bibliography is divided into four sections: the history and technique of blacksmithing, individual craftsmen, exhibition catalogues, and periodicals. It is based on the booklist compiled for *Forging Iron*, the International Conference and Workshop organised by the Crafts Council at Hereford Technical College and Ironbridge Gorge Museum, from 22 until 28 July, 1980. Whilst a number of the books are now out of print, numerous books on blacksmithing are held by the National Art Library, Victoria & Albert Museum, and by Brunel University, Shoreditch Campus Library. Books in print are indicated*.

History and technique

ALEXANDER, W. & STREET, A.: *Metals in the Service of Man*, Harmondsworth, Pelican, 1976.
A classic early Pelican account of the science of metals for the general reader.

ANDREWS, Jack: *The Edge of the Anvil*, Emmans, Pa., Kodale Press, 1977.
A basic resource book covering every technical aspect of wrought ironwork, photographs of the work of Samuel Yellin, and a good bibliography.

ANGIER, R.H.: *Firearm Blueing and Browning*, Harrisburg, Pa., The Stackpole Co., n.d.,
Contains many formulae for surface colouring.

BELGIUM, Ministère de la culture française: *Bruxelles, 1890-1975: guide d'architecture*, Brussels, La Conti, 1976.
A useful architectural guide to Brussels, including a map, pinpointing the location of many outstanding examples of Art Nouveau ironwork.

*CoSIRA: *The Blacksmith's Craft Technique*. London, CoSIRA, 1976.
An excellent manual of instruction, 37 graded lessons.

*DILLAMORE, I.L.: *Some metallurgy intended for blacksmiths*, Forging Iron Conference Papers, London, Crafts Council, p.p., 1980.

EDWARDS, Ifor: *Davies Brothers, Gatesmiths*, Welsh Arts Council/Crafts Council, 1977.
An illustrated study of Robert Davies and his brother, 18th century Welsh smiths.

FERRARI, G.: *Il ferro nell'arte Italiano*, 3rd ed., Milan, 1910.

FISHLOCK, David: *Metal colouring*, London, Robert Draper Ltd., 1962.

FLEURY, Gaston: *Le fer forgé dans la decoration moderne, extérieurs et intérieurs*, Paris, C. Massin & Co., 1923.

GEERLINGS, G.K.: *Wrought Iron in Architecture*, New York, Charles Scribner, 1929.
Excellent illustrations including examples of the work of Yellin and other great American smiths. Also covers European smiths.

GOODWIN-SMITH, R.: *English Domestic Metalwork*, Leigh on Sea, F. Lewis Ltd., 1937.
A private press publication written by a designer; good photographs. Especially good on 1930s ornamental metalwork of all kinds; reference list of metalworkers of the time.

GRUNDY ARNATT Ltd.: *Architectural Metalwork*, Hampton Wick, Kingston-on-Thames, Grundy Arnatt Ltd., n.d.

*HARRIS, John: *English Decorative Ironwork from contemporary source books 1610-1836*, London, Alec Tiranti, 1960.
A selection of drawings from original source books, including Tijou's 'A New Booke of Drawings'.

*HARTLEY, Dorothy: *Made in England*, London, Eyre Methuen, 1939; 4th ed., 1974.
In the mid 1930s, Dorothy Hartley, trained as an engineer, travelled with her camera and notebook in search of craftsmen at work. Her book contains thorough accounts of various crafts past and present.

HENRIOT, Gabriel: *La Ferronnerie moderne*, Paris 1928.

HOEVER, Otto: *A Handbook of wrought iron from the Middle Ages to the end of the eighteenth century*, London, Thames & Hudson Ltd., 1962.

HOFFMAN, Gretl and MAURACH, Jurgen: *Schmiede-und Schlosserarbeiten von heute*, Stuttgart, Julius Hoffmann, n.d.
West German forged work of the early 1970s; very well illustrated.

*LILLICO, J.W.: *Blacksmiths' Manual Illustrated*, Technical Press Ltd., 1930; new ed., 1978.
Useful on the making and use of power hammer tools for forging.

LINDSAY, J. Seymour: *An Anatomy of English Wrought Iron 1000-1800AD*, London, Alec Tiranti, 1964.
Remarkable drawings of ironwork, illustrating technique.

LINDSAY, J. Seymour: *Iron and Brass Implements of the English House*, London, Alex Tiranti 1964.

LISTER, Reymond: *Decorative Wrought in Great Britain*, London, G. Bell & Sons, 1957; reprint: Newton Abbot, David & Charles, 1970.
A very good introduction to tools, materials and techniques, followed by a historical survey of British ironwork.

MAGNANI, Franco: *Ornamental metalwork*, New York, Universe Books, 1967.
Photographs of contemporary Italian and Swiss metalwork.

MARTINIE, Henri: *Exposition des arts decoratifs, Paris, 1925: La ferronnerie*, Paris, 1926.

MEILACH, Dona Z.: *Decorative and sculptural ironwork: tools, technique and inspiration*, New York, Crown Publishers Inc., 1977.
Very good photographs, showing a wide range of modern American work; the text although stimulating cannot always be trusted technically.

MEYER, F.S.: *A handbook of art smithing*, translated from the 2nd and enlarged German edition, with an introduction by J. Starkie Gardner. New York, 1896.

MINAMIZAWA, Hiroshi: *Wrought Iron*, Yoshiyo Kobo Laboratory, 1976.
The only book on wrought iron published in Japan by a Japanese smith.

MOORE, Thomas: *Handbook of practical smithing and forging*, London E. & F.N. Spon Ltd., 1941.
A useful book for the wrought iron student, giving information on industrial smiths' work.

NIALL, Ian: *Country blacksmith*, London, 1966.

PERRIN, G.M.: *La ferronerie française contemporaine*, 1961.

RIVERDALE, Lord: *Hints to practical users of tool steel*, Sheffield, Arthur Balfour & Co., n.d.
Particularly good on forging carbon steels for tool making.

ROTH, Edwin: *Neue Schmiedeformen*, Munich, Callwey Verlag, 1962.
Most of the work in this influential book consists of work designed by Roth and made up by craftsmen under his direction; fully illustrated.

SCHEEL, Hans: *Schmiede und Schlosserarbeiten: Gestaltete Arbeiten aus Stahl, Sondermessing, und Leichtemetall*, 1959; 2 vols.

*SCHMIRLER, Otto: *The Art of wrought metalwork for house and garden*. London, Harrap, 1980.
500 drawings and over 200 photographs illustrate the author's work; text in English, French and German.

SCHUBERT, H.R.: *History of the British iron and steel industry from c.45BC to AD1775*, London, Routledge & Kegan Paul, 1957.

*STARKIE GARDNER, J.: *English ironwork of the 17th and 18th centuries*, London, B.T. Batsford 1911; facsimile reprint: New York, Amo Press Inc., 1976.
The classic account of the development of English ironwork, written by a practising smith.

*STARKIE GARDNER, J.: *Ironwork*, London, H.M.S.O.,1922, reprinted in 1978, (3 volumes.)
An excellent survey, although not all attributions are reliable; useful supplementary bibliography.

TSCHERNEK, Willi & BERGMEISTER, Manfred: *Entwurfe Seitnäher Schmiedearbeiten*, Lübeck, Coleman Verlag & Bad Worishofen, Holzmann Verlag.

WEBBER, Ronald: *The village blacksmith*, Newton Abbott, David & Charles, 1971.

*WEYGERS, Alexander G.: *The making of tools*, Van Nostrand Reinhold, 1977; paperback.
How to make and sharpen blacksmith's tools.

*WEYGERS, Alexander G.: *The modern blacksmith*, Van Nostrand Reinhold, 1974.
This discusses the range of techniques involved in blacksmithing.

WOLF, Fridolin: *Kunstschmieden in Beispielen*, Lübeck, Coleman Verlag, 1979.

WOLF, Fridolin: *Kunstschmiedepraxis*, Lübeck, Coleman Verlag, 1975.

Wrought iron railings, doors and gates, An Architect and Building News Book, Architects' 'Detail' Library, vol. 1. London, Iliffe Books Ltd., 1966.

Wrought iron: European household utensils from the 17th to the 19th century, catalogue 1975 Art Gallery of Ontario, Canada: travelling exhibition.
Items featured from the MacDonald Stewart collection, Montreal Military & Maritime Museum; includes references to wrought iron collections which may be seen by the public.

ZIMBELLI, Umberto & VERGIO, Giovanni: *Decorative ironwork*, London, Hamlyn 1966.

References to individual craftsmen

BENETTON, Simon:
Salvatore Mangeri: *Simon*, catalogue of an exhibition held at the Galleria d'Arte Moderna San Marco, Bassano del Grappa, February 1981.
Simon Benetton, Commenti di Carlo Munari, (with other contributors), Genoa, Immordino Editore, n.d.

BENETTON, Toni:
Franco Batachi: *Schmiedeeisen für Haus und Garten: Prof. Benetton*, Tübingen, Wasmuth Verlay, 1970.
Gabriele Mandel & L.G. Bortolato: *Toni Benetton*, Treviso, 1970.

BERGMEISTER, German & Manfred:
Stahl und Form, Kunstschmiedearbeiten, Düsseldorf, Verlag Stahleisen, n.d.

BRANDT, Edgar:
Gabriel Mourey: 'Edgar Brandt, the French ironworker', *The Studio*, 1926, vol. 91, pp. 33-335.
Ferrobrandt Inc., New York, 1926.
Edmond Uhry: 'Edgar Brandt', *Art et Décoration*, 1909, vol. 25. pp. 45-52.
Paul Essenbrey: 'Brandt, Master ironworker, a great French craftsman', *The International Studio*, vol. 80, 1924, pp. 253-258.

BUTLER, Reg:
Robert Melville: 'Personnages in Iron', *Architectural Review*, CVIII, 1951, pp. 147-151.

HORTA, Victor:
Franco Borsi, *Victor Horta*, with contributions by Paulo Portughesi, Brussels, Vokaer, 1970.

KÜHN, Fritz:
Metaux façonnés de Fritz Kühn, catalogue of an exhibition held at the Musée des Arts Decoratifs, Paris, 17 April – 12 May 1969.
Decorative work in wrought iron and other metals, London, George C. Harrap, 1967.
This book consists mainly of photographs, working drawings and captions, exploring the extremely wide range of Kuhn's work.
Eisen und Stahl, Leipzig, 1957.
Geschmiedes Gerät (Forged utensils), Tübingen, Wasmuth Verlag, 3rd ed., 1967.
Stahl Gestaltung: Entwurfslehre des Kunst-Schmiedens (Forming Steel: Design Principles for the Artist Blacksmith), Tübingen, Ernst Wasmuth, 1956.
Photographs of finished work with plans, drawings and design sketches.
Stahl und Metall Arbeiten von Fritz Kuhn, Tübingen, Ernst Wasmuth Verlag, 1959.

*MACKINTOSH, Charles Rennie:
Charles Rennie Mackintosh: Ironwork and Metalwork at Glasgow School of Art, selected and described by H. Jefferson Barnes, p.p., Glasgow, Glasgow School of Art, 2nd ed. with revisions, 1978. (Available from Glasgow School of Art.)

MAZZUCOTELLI, Alessandro: Rossana Bossaglia & Arno Hammacher:
Mazzucotelli, Milan, Edizioni Il Polifili, 1971.

PALEY, Albert:
'Craft in Architecture: Albert Paley's Albany Gates', *American Craft*, vol. 41, no 2, April/May 1981, pp. 18-19.
The Metalwork of Albert Paley, catalogue of an exhibition held at the John Michael Kohler Arts Center, Sheboygan, Wisconsin, April 13 – June 1980; Hunter Museum of Art, Chattanooga, Tennessee, October 19 – November 23, 1980.
Robert A. Sobieszek, 'Albert Paley, Romantic in Metal', *American Craft*, vol. 40, no. 2, April/May 1980, pp. 12–17, 83.
Paley, Castle, Windenhaim, catalogue of an exhibition held at the Memorial Art Gallery of the University of Rochester, August 24 – October 7, 1979.

ROBERT, Emile:
P.P. Calmettes, 'Un maître ferronnier, Emile Robert', *Art et Décoration*, vol. 23, 1908, pp. 89-98.

SUBES, Raymond:
Henri Clouzot, *Raymond Subes, maître ferronnier, dernières oeuvres. . .* Paris, 1931.

YELLIN, Samuel:
Costen Fitz-gibbon, 'Decorative ironwork within the house, with examples taken from the work of Samuel Yellin, craftsman, *Arts & Decoration*, vol. 4, 1914, pp. 307-9.
W.B. McCormick, 'Samuel Yellin, artist in iron', *The International Studio*, no. 2, vol. 75, pp. 430-434.

Exhibition catalogues (alphabetical order)

The Blacksmith, An exhibition 1972-3; Pennsylvania Farm Museum, Pennsylvania Historical and Museum Commission 1976, Harrisburg, Pa.

The Craftsman's Art, an exhibition of new work by British craftsmen at the Victoria & Albert Museum, London, Crafts Advisory Committee, 1973.

Tools from the 17th to the 19th century, Flint Institute of Arts, De Waters Art Center, Michigan, 26 April – 7 June, 1981.

Iron, Solid Wrought/USA, an exhibition assembled by Evert Johnson celebrating the theme: the Blacksmith as Artist and Craftsman in the United States, 1776-1976. Southern Illinois University at Carboldale, Carbondale, Illinois, September 27 – October 20, 1976.

Jewellery in Europe, a touring exhibition of progressive work selected by Ralph Turner, organised by the Scottish Arts Council and the Crafts Advisory Committee, 1975-1976, catalogue published by the Scottish Arts Council, Edinburgh.

Kunstausstellung Eisen und Stahl, Kuratorium Kunstausstellung, Düsseldorf, 1952. Catalogue introduction by Dr. Werner Doede.

**Kunstschmiedearbeit heute,* Internationale Ausstellung in Lindau/Bodensee. Altes Rathaus – Cavazzen – Freigelande Stadtpark, 19 July – 21 September 1969.

**Kunstschmiedearbeit heute,* Internationale Ausstellung in Lindau/Bodensee, Altes Rathaus – Cavazzen – Freigelande Stadtpark. 12 June – 1 September 1974.

Made of Iron (exhibition . . . assembled as a contribution to the Arts Festival of Houston), University of St. Thomas, Art Department, Houston, Texas, 1966.

**The Maker's Eye,* London, Crafts Council, 1982.

**Moderne Kunstschmiedearbeiten und Skulpturen,* Internationale Ausstellung in Lindau/Bodensee Halle an der Zwanzigerstrasse, Fussgangerzone, Stadtpark, 23 May – 10 September 1980. The catalogue of this most recent part of the international series of ironwork exhibitions at Lindau is available from: Herr Blumel, Fachverband Metall Bayern, 8 Munchen 5, Erhardstrasse 6, West Germany.

Periodicals

American Crafts   (Monthly)
P.O. Box 561, Martinsville, N.J. 08836, U.S.A.

The Anvil's Ring   (Quarterly)
The journal of the Artist Blacksmiths' Association of North America (ABANA), membership of which includes a subscription to the journals. Details from: Dr. Carl Van Arnam, ABANA Secretary-Treasurer, P.O. Box 1191, Gainesville, Florida 32602, U.S.A., from whom back copies are also available. This lively magazine combines reviews of current work by ABANA members, with articles on history and technique, and a well-informed events calendar.

Architectural Design   (Monthly)
7/8 Holland Street, London W8

Architects' Journal   (Weekly)
9/13 Queen Anne's Gate, London SW1H 9BY

Architectural Review   (Monthly)
9/13 Queen Anne's Gate, London SW1H 9BY

The British Blacksmith   (Quarterly)
The newsletter of the British Artist Blacksmiths Association (BABA), founded in 1977, free to members. Details from: Richard Quinnell, Secretary, BABA, Rowhurst Forge, Oxshott Road, Leatherhead, Surrey.

Building Design   (Weekly)
Calderwood Street, London SW18.

Country Life   (Weekly)
IPC Magazines Ltd., Kings Reach Tower, Stamford Street, London SE1 9LS.

Crafts   (Bi-monthly)
The Crafts Council, 8 Waterloo Place, London SW1Y 4AT.

Design   (Monthly)
The Design Council, 28 Haymarket, London SW1Y 4SU.

Domus   (11 issues p.a.)
Centro Domus, Via Manzoni 37, 20121 Milan, Italy.

House & Garden   (Monthly)
Vogue House, Hanover Square, London W1.

Interiors   (Monthly
228-230 Fulham Road, London SW10 9NB.

Journal of the Royal Institute of British Architects   (Monthly)
Royal Institute of British Architects, 66 Portland Place, London W1.